# Stuck in the Shallow End

# Stuck in the Shallow End

## Education, Race, and Computing

**Jane Margolis**
Rachel Estrella
Joanna Goode
Jennifer Jellison Holme
Kimberly Nao

The MIT Press
Cambridge, Massachusetts
London, England

MIT Press books may be purchased at special quantity discounts for business or sales promotional use. For information, please email <special_sales@mitpress.mit.edu> or write to Special Sales Department, The MIT Press, 55 Hayward Street, Cambridge, MA 02142.

This book was set in Sabon by Graphic Composition, Inc. Printed and bound in the United States of America.

Library of Congress Cataloging-in-Publication Data

Margolis, Jane.
Stuck in the shallow end : education, race, and computing / Jane Margolis with Rachel Estrella . . . [et al.].
   p.   cm.
Includes bibliographical references and index.
ISBN 978-0-262-13504-7 (hardcover : alk. paper)
1. Computer science—study and teaching (Secondary)—United States. 2. Children of minorities—Education (Secondary)—United States. 3. Digital divide—United States. I. Title.
QA76.27.M347   2008
004.071—dc22

2008013827

10  9  8  7  6  5  4  3  2  1

# Contents

# Foreword

Shirley Malcom

When I agreed to read and comment on *Stuck in the Shallow End: Education, Race, and Computing*, I could not have imagined that a research-based document could have stirred such visceral reactions—from sorrow to rage, from despair to hope. The book tells stories: about the struggle of young people to make a place for themselves in a knowledge-based economy through the study of computing; about expectations and assumptions of capacity based on the race, gender, or social class of students; about the personal interactions of students and teachers or students with each other that preserve a stratified intellectual class system; and about the unintended consequences of well intentioned policies at every level.

While *Stuck in the Shallow End* is ostensibly about access and denial of access to high school–level courses in computer science based on race, sex, and socioeconomic status, it is also a larger treatise on the potential and reality of education to remove barriers and to support social and economic equality. The authors relate the outcomes of their examination of courses and course taking at three high schools that differed widely by demographics, and advertised and real access to programs in computer science. The study of computer science can be seen as a possible route to future economic opportunity. Yet we are shown three different examples of where local, state, and national circumstances conspired in a "perfect storm" to reinforce entrenchment of privilege and intellectual impoverishment. Lack of authentic access gets translated into victim blaming while preparatory privilege gets translated into a "gift for computing," yielding the ultimate self-fulfilling prophecy.

Hope was stirred when the authors shifted roles from observers to change agents, seeking to address some of the structural problems feeding the inequalities. As they started with the teachers, seeking to create a learning community, helping to bring more energy and creativity to their teaching, and bringing university colleagues on board, I cheered their decisions to become involved. But as I continued to read, my worst fears were realized—shifts in personnel, external policy pressures, and other circumstances yielded a loss of ground. Yet, ultimately, hope was sustained by the knowledge that local actions can make a difference. Now it is up to the rest of us to affect the policy environments—local, state, and federal—so that system transformation is possible.

I thought long and hard about why I had such a reaction to this book. Perhaps it was because, even though my background is in the life sciences, so much of it felt like my own story—a highly motivated, reasonably intelligent student in a terribly under-resourced school in the segregated South. Moving to college where I was "the only" in so many classes, I identified with the student who felt the need to "represent," to be present and to do well, even while knowing that I had to run harder to catch up and keep up. I knew what it was like to be "lost" in class but unwilling to ask questions in that setting and labeled as dumb, and to finally reach out for help knowing that I was not dumb but under-prepared. I was fortunate to find the intellectual and social supports to stay with it until I could gain my footing. And once that happened I was able to move into the deep end of the pool.

That is the challenge that lies ahead. Now that we know the barriers can we begin to address them? Can we take the existing educational system that, according to economist Isabel Sawhill of the Brookings Institution, reinforces the status quo and change it to one that offers real opportunity? The answers lie with us, in our willingness to speak truth to those in power, to accept nothing less than *real* opportunities for all children, and to take on the responsibilities to be true to our democratic ideals. No matter where students begin, we must not let their aspirations die in the shallow end of the pool.

# Acknowledgments

This book has been made possible through years of conversation and deep partnerships.

Without the ongoing support of key people in the Los Angeles Unified School District (LAUSD) we would not have been welcomed into the schools for our research and, later, our partnership programs. Specifically, Dr. Todd Ullah, director of secondary science for the LAUSD, John Kwan, Dr. Themy Sparangis, and Dr. Diane Watkins have lent invaluable support for developing more computer science learning opportunities in Los Angeles schools. The LAUSD teachers have provided us with insights and demonstrated a remarkable commitment to teaching in their schools. We are particularly thankful to the teachers who have allowed us to share their stories in this book and for those who have participated in the summer institute and AP Readiness program for their willingness to devote their time and energy to increase access to computer science for underrepresented students. This book is a testament to the conditions they face, and the tireless work they do on a daily basis. But, it is for the LAUSD students and others around the country that we write. We watch with respect as they continuously navigate a system that is filled with obstacles, that is not providing them with what they deserve. Their strength and determination are models of accomplishment.

Years of intellectual guidance and collaboration with colleagues at the Institute for Democracy, Education, and Access at the University of California at Los Angeles (UCLA) have helped us frame our thoughts, think through what we were discovering, and how we were to present our findings. We are most grateful for the years of conversation with Jeannie Oakes, John Rogers, Marisa Saunders, Karen Quartz, Jesse Moya, and recently Sophie Fanelli. Our frame for thinking about computer science education has been deeply informed by the pioneering research done by Jeannie Oakes on school tracking and inequality in the schools. We are also grateful for the support we received from Jerchel Anderson, Nery Orellana, and Jared Planas of IDEA. Also at UCLA, we would like to thank Priscilla Lee, director of UCLA's AP Readiness program, who has advocated tirelessly for support programs for LAUSD students, and because of her work, many students have increased opportunities to learn rigorous mathematics and science content.

Inspirational and breakthrough meetings about our findings and the framing of the book took place with Allan Fisher (who went beyond the call of duty), Mike Rose, Margaret Eisenhart, Justine Cassell, Simeon Stumme, and other members of our Advisory Committee: Claude Steele, Danny Solórzano, Janet Schofield. Further pivotal conversations and readings of draft chapters were done by: Brigid Barron, Maureen Biggers, Alison Clark, Wayne Coffey, John Cruzat, Penny Eckert, Barb Ericson, Juan Gilbert, Mark Guzdial, Pattie Heyman, Sheila Humphries, Yasmin Kafai, Shirley Malcom, Beryl Minkle, Mia Ong, Debra Satz, Lisa Sjostrom, Chris Stephenson, Richard Tapia, Mark Warschauer, and Andrew Williams. Several UCLA graduate and undergraduate students helped us shape this project and collect data: Yvonne de la Pena, Menaka Fernando, and Karlene Nguyen. We are fortunate to have had such a remarkable group of friends and scholars helping us in this work.

Though there are five authors of this book, it is clear how many more people have contributed to this project, and volunteered their time to read and review various chapters. The finished product is testimony to their feedback, although we ultimately take responsibility for our statements and how we have shaped this book. We cannot overemphasize the contributions of Karen Jarsky, who entered late in the project, but was able to take the numerous threads of our ideas and help us weave them into a seamless whole with such commitment and care, unifying our five voices. Her editing skills deepened our writing and helped our story come alive. And thank you to the MIT Press, specifically Bob Prior and Susan Buckley, who have both offered consistent support and patience as we worked to wrap up this project.

Without the support and advice of Caroline Wardle and Jan Cuny of the National Science Foundation (NSF), this work would not have been possible. Caroline offered consistent support for years, and Jan's vision of community building, galvanizing a diverse grouping of scholars across the nation in the Broadening the Participation in Computing program of the NSF, has introduced us to other scholars across the country, both computer scientists and social scientists, who have deepened our understanding of these issues.

Other communities we have learned so much from, and have been supported by are the Grace Hopper Celebration of Women in Computing, the Richard Tapia Celebration of Diversity in Computing, and the National Center for Women in Information Technology (NCWIT). The NCWIT leadership team (Lucy Sanders, Bobby Schnabel, Telle Whitney, Lecia Barker, and Joanne McGrath Cohoon) have been willing to go the mile in trying to keep our work afloat when it has been threatened by various funding crises. We are eternally grateful to Chris Stephenson, leader of the NCWIT K–12 Alliance and executive director of the Computer Science Teachers Association. Chris is a fount of wisdom and a most generous partner in this work.

From the UCLA Henry Samueli School of Engineering and Applied Science, Dean Vijay Dhir has contributed resources and support. David Smallberg, a committed and outstanding UCLA computer science lecturer, has spent many years helping us work with the LAUSD teachers and students. This work could not have been done without him.

Two additional sources of inspiration for us have been the Spelbots, Spellman College's robotics team, and the Richard Tapia "Math Is Cool" team at Rice University. We are grateful to both for their willingness to talk with us and travel to Los Angeles to present their work, their passion, and themselves to LAUSD students and teachers.

Thank you to Google and the Alfred B. Sloan Foundation. We are particularly indebted to Ted Greenwood of the Sloan Foundation, and Allan Eustace and Jeff Walz of Google, who provided the necessary support to keep the book writing alive. Our research and partnership-building work in the LAUSD has also been supported financially by additional organizations, including Microsoft, Intel, Boeing, Northrop-Grumman, and UCLA's Center for Community Partnerships.

And then, we are grateful for each other, for this has been a extraordinary friendship and collaboration over many years. We have also received support from those around us, particularly our immediate family members: Mark Peterson, Sophie Margolis-Peterson, Brian Kowal, Kai Estrella-Kowal, Jason Sydes, Troy Holme, Katie and Anna Holme, and Kadar Vernes. All have been patient and self-sacrificing as we spent many preoccupied moments away.

To end, Jane would like to make a special dedication of this book to her parents, Jules and Doris Margolis, who insisted that their daughter put the completion of this book before their own extremely pressing needs, and who have demonstrated to all who know them how to live a life defined by commitment to family, friends, and the entire world.

# Stuck in the Shallow End

# Introduction

## The Myth of Technology as the "Great Equalizer"

This book reports the findings of a study investigating why so few African American and Latino/a high school students are learning computer science. Yet unexpectedly, our perspective was sharpened toward the end of the research project by stumbling on a newspaper article about a program designed to teach more African American children to swim. The *New York Times* article, titled "Everyone into the Water" (Zinser 2006), was accompanied by a large color photograph of children of different races by the side of a pool. It described the program at a fitness center tucked away on the Upper East Side of Manhattan, Asphalt Green, where "for at least one day a year, the overwhelmingly white world of swimming gets turned on its ear." Asphalt Green sponsors the "Big Swim," the culmination of a larger program fighting to close the racial gap in swimming. Our thinking about what we observed in our study of why so few African American and Latino/a students are learning computer science would never be the same after reading this article.

We recognized swimming as a sport with mostly white athletes, but it was the article's subtitle, "Closing Swimming's Deadly Racial Gap," and the statistics in the opening paragraph that grabbed our attention: African American children are as much as *three times more likely* than white children to drown.[1] This number shocked us and disrupted our linear pattern of thinking. The issue was not solely about integrating another activity such as tennis or skiing, or for that matter computer science. Because of the racial gap in swimming, some children lose their lives.

The article went on to explain how the racial gap in swimming was born during slavery, continued on through the violence of Jim Crow, and has created a world of higher numbers of African American children drowning as well as a competitive sport that is "bereft of minorities." But what was the historical connection all the way back to slavery? And how had this persisted for so many years? We began to read all we could to learn more about the history of swimming, the reasons behind these tragic drowning statistics, and why swimming continues to be a "white sport."

We share what we learned about these issues in chapter 1, because they have become for us a big part of the "why we write this book." We were appalled when we learned about the historical legacy that follows swimming today, the toll it has taken—not only on the African American community, but also on other communities of color—and the belief systems that have arisen over the years to justify the segregated state of this sport. Simultaneously, the themes that emerged from the history of swimming segregation clarified for us the larger patterns we were seeing in our study of computer science. The unexpected parallels between segregation in swimming and underrepresentation in computer science then became the central metaphor of our work.

To be sure, computer science and swimming are vastly different activities—swimming is a physical activity with a long and violent past, and computer science is a cognitive activity and one that has emerged in the post–civil rights era—but the race gaps in the two arenas are parallel in many ways. The study of each field shows how access denied, combined with belief systems that rationalize this lack of access, translate—over the short and long term—into inequalities in knowledge, interest, and ultimately participation. And while a lack of participation may at first appear benign, closer study reveals the harm that can come from it. So the more we can learn by seeing the same processes at work across varied and dramatically different activities, the more insights we obtain about inequality and segregation, and how they are fueled in our society.

This, then, explains our title. Through our study of why so few African Americans and Latino/as are learning computer science, we have learned how in computer science, as in swimming, people of color have been denied access (and in the case of swimming, *violently* so) to facilities, resources, and critical learning opportunities. Further, in both cases, the underrepresentation is rationalized, and made to seem as if it is based on a "natural sorting" process of innate propensities and capabilities, instead of deep structural inequities (Kao 2000). As a result, lives continue to be at risk, and in education as in swimming, too many young people are tragically and unconscionably "stuck in the shallow end."

Our investigation at three Los Angeles high schools reveals how these inequities are created and reproduced. We identify "virtual segregation" as an insidious phenomenon that occurs when we are led to believe that we are moving toward equality, and pretend that everyone has a chance and a choice. In reality the histories have been so different, the playing fields so uneven, the chasm so deep and wide, that people are living in two different worlds, receiving two different and very unequal types of educations, opportunities, and levels of knowledge.

## A Lens on a Much Larger Issue

We are talking with Jontille, an African American eleventh grader, about why so few African American and Latino/a students are enrolled in computer science classes at her predominantly African American Los Angeles public high school.[2] "The minorities—Hispanics, African American kids," she surmises, "they're not really interested in it." Reflecting on the issue a bit longer, however, Jontille digs deeper to detect an underlying cause, adding:

But I think that's only because they haven't been really shown how to work with computers. So, therefore, their interest lies elsewhere. But I noticed that a lot of the Caucasian students, they're into technology, and a lot of the Asian students [too]. . . . But I think that if they [African American and Hispanics] knew that they had more access to it, that they would do it, you know?

Her friend, Nia, also African American, offers another perspective on the racial and ethnic makeup of the world of computing: "I think minorities are . . . are scared, you know, to jump into the future because what it looks like is only Caucasians should be in that industry."

Jontille and Nia are 2 of the 185 students we interviewed for our study into why so few African American and Latino/a high school students are learning computer science. The responses and narratives provided by these students as well as their teachers raise fundamental questions about inherent interest, access to resources and appropriate classes, images of a field like computer science, and issues of race and ethnicity. These are issues we worked to understand and disentangle in our investigation of who does—and does not—study computer science.

Commenting further about "not knowing enough" about computers, Jontille reflects on what this means: "I think I'm going to have to take another computer class because . . . with all the technology moving so fast, I don't know enough. I don't know enough about computers, I think, and I think I'm going to get left behind in that area and I do not want to be behind."

Technology is "moving so fast." Computer science is a discipline that is serving as a critical instrument of innovation from the sciences to the arts, and it is transforming the ways we live our personal and professional lives. Despite the centrality of computer hardware and software development in today's world, only a narrow and exclusive band of our population is learning the skills and techniques imparted by computer science. Why is this the case?

Starting in 2000, we were funded by the National Science Foundation (NSF) to investigate why so few African American and Latino/a high school students were studying computer science.[3] The NSF was concerned about the underrepresentation of minority students in the field, and the overall drop in the interest and numbers of students studying the subject.[4] We are not computer scientists but rather a team of social scientists, long committed to understanding the factors that undermine equity in education. We were drawn to identifying the sources of these particular instructional disparities at a time when educational and economic opportunities are increasingly intertwined with computer science, and in an era when the youths of all races and genders are virtually dependent on the use of technology for their entertainment and social lives.

The story we tell takes place in three different schools in Los Angeles. The first school is an extremely overcrowded facility in East Los Angeles with an almost entirely Latino/a student population. The second one is an aerospace mathematics science magnet in mid–Los Angeles with a predominantly African American population. In both of these schools with high numbers of students of color, only introductory computing courses covering basic low-level "cut-and-paste" skills are currently available. Our third site is a neighborhood school surrounded by mansions overlooking the Pacific Ocean. Even though it is located in a white and wealthy community, two-thirds of the school population are students of color who travel from all over Los Angeles to attend this well-funded campus. Unlike our first two schools, students here have opportunities to study computer science beyond basic introductory skills; there is a relatively wide array of computing-related courses, including college-preparatory Advanced Placement (AP) classes. Yet we soon notice that even though advanced computing courses are available, few students of color at the school are enrolled in them.

Computing is the kind of high-status knowledge that taps a student into the grid of twenty-first-century opportunities. It is tempting to think that because it is a technical activity, it should be free of the biases that affect more obviously culturally situated fields like business or law. Nevertheless, few students of color are "choosing" to learn computer science at all three of these schools, even those students who are in a setting where the courses are offered. What is going on here?

Our research took place as politicians and policymakers were increasingly worried about the overall decline in interest as well as expertise in mathematics and science in the United States, fearful that America was losing its innovative edge.[5] We approached this question a bit differently, following the perspective of mathematics educator Robert Moses that the knowledge gap in math, science, and technology could turn students of color into the "designated serfs of the information age" (Moses and Cobb 2002, 11), and that this is a civil rights issue for the twenty-first century.[6] We believe that opportunities to learn computer science, independent of its value as a stepping-stone to proficiency in an age of technology, are indicative of opportunity more broadly defined.

This recognition of the importance of computer science was a central motivator for us as we undertook this project, especially at the outset. Then, as often happens in research projects such as this, as we went deeper into our subject, issues began to emerge that suggested a much larger story than we had originally intended. We soon realized that our study of the "computer science pipeline" was a lens into what Jonathan Kozol (1992) more broadly refers to as the "savage inequalities" in our schools. Specifically, our research was revealing how students of color in low-resourced schools are much more generally being denied the learning opportunities and preparation they need and deserve for the changing economic reality of the twenty-first century. Our research also was revealing how inequality gets produced in our society.

As we observed the daily details of inequality unfolding, we realized the broader implications of what we were witnessing as well. The mechanisms and beliefs that channel students of color away from computer science do the same thing in other areas of high-status knowledge.[7] The end result is that students of color by and large are being denied a wide range of occupational or educational futures. And so we ultimately came at our research question with another motivation: to reveal the much broader implications of these computer science inequities. To the extent that there is a race gap in this field, and to the extent that there are disparities in access to and the quality of educational opportunities, our inquiry tells us much about the state of our educational institutions, and how schools are limiting the reach and achievement of their students. Therefore, in the end, it can be fairly stated that our book is not really about computer science. Or better said, it is about computer science, but it is also about a lot more.

Before we can move into these broader issues, we must first establish the current state of computer science, and the statistics reveal the depth of the racial and ethnic divide in the field. A recent survey showed that at the nation's PhD-granting departments of computer science and engineering, just 8 percent of the bachelor's degrees and 4 percent of the master's degrees in computer science are awarded to African Americans and Latino/as (Zweben 2006). In California, where underrepresented students of color make up a combined 49 percent of the high school student population, they account for only 9 percent of the AP computer science test takers (California Department of Education 2005; College Entrance Examination Board 2005). These statistics are especially disturbing in a minority-majority state that gave rise to and nurtures Silicon Valley and houses several of the nation's top computer science programs. Given these statistics, the question we ask is obvious: How does this field remain segregated in the midst of so much professed concern about the problem? Before we can answer that question, we must first more clearly explain what we mean by computer science.

### What Is Computer Science, Anyway?

Often when people hear about our research, they assume that we are investigating students' learning of computer *literacy* skills such as word processing or Internet and Web searching. These literacy skills are without a doubt a twenty-first-century necessity, and all endeavors in schools and communities to assure all citizens access to these skills are critically important. But we are looking beyond computer literacy skills, and instead examining who is and is not learning computer *science*. So what is computer science, anyway? Succinctly—albeit broadly—defined, "computer science (CS) is the study of computers and algorithmic processes, including their principles, their hardware and software designs, their applications, and their impact on society" (ACM K–12 Task Force Curriculum Committee 2003, 6).

An algorithm, in simple terms, can be understood as a list of well-defined instructions for accomplishing a task. Within the context of computer science, algorithms take the form of computer programs, and are essentially the language with which we tell computers what we want them to do and how they should do it. Therefore, in lay language, one could say that there is a problem-solving process at the foundation of computer science. The complexity and analytic thinking involved in this process is valuable to know within as well as across an increasing number of professions.

A "users' guide" for Stanford University computer science majors describes how computer science is a remarkably young field, yet a revolutionary one:

It was just over fifty years ago that the first electronic computers were developed, and there was no recognition at the time of computer science as a field of study separate from electrical engineering or mathematics. Over time, as computers became increasingly powerful and were applied to more and more tasks, people began to realize that the task of programming those computers to solve problems was an extremely difficult problem requiring theories and practice unlike those used in existing fields. Computer science—the science of solving problems with the aid of a computer—became a new discipline in its own right.[8]

This new discipline is now having a seismic impact across disciplines and professions. In an article titled "All Science Is Computer Science," author George Johnson (2001) writes about computer science in the twenty-first century: "As research on so many fronts is becoming increasingly dependent on computation, all science, it seems, is becoming computer science." While we are not prepared to argue that all science is becoming computer science, there is no doubt that computer science is having a transformative impact across all walks of life, and that it is key to innovation across the world. Occupations, industries, and undertakings as diverse as HIV and influenza research, air safety, psychological inquiry, the elimination of world hunger, studies of the world's climate, and the Human Genome Project, just to name a few, would all be crippled without the benefit of computer science. On a grand scale, computer science is transforming knowledge and the scientific questions that can be investigated.[9]

It is not just science that is being transformed. In the creative arts, the changes brought on by computation are also sweeping. Motion pictures today are a "window into an ungodly amount of computation and engineering innovation and talent" (Taub 2003). With each new round of film releases, the use of technology ratchets up even more. The same transformations are happening in music and theater, where advanced technologies are used in set design, lighting, and many aspects of staging for large-scale productions. Similarly, graphic designers, whose tool kits once consisted of paper and pencils, must now have significant technological expertise to make a living at their art.

In her widely circulated thought piece called "Computational Thinking" (2006), Jeannette Wing, the director of the NSF's Computer and Information Sciences and Engineering Division, has coined a phrase in an attempt to further define computer science. As described on the Carnegie Mellon School of Computer Science Web site, "Computational thinking is a way of solving problems, designing systems, and understanding human behavior that draws on concepts fundamental to computer science. Computational thinking is thinking in terms of abstractions, invariably multiple layers of abstraction at once. Computational thinking is about the automation of these abstractions."[10] In her role at the NSF, Wing aspires to change the image of computing for the general public and increase the understanding that often without us even realizing it, computing touches our daily lives. She wants to inspire everyone to learn computational thinking, to have the tools that computer science offers, because computer science is now integral to and enhances many professions, whether in computer science or elsewhere.[11]

Not only is overwhelming job growth in information technology and engineering projected over the next decade; computer science is one of the keys to innovation in general.[12] Thomas Friedman (2005), in his best-selling book *The World Is Flat*, argues, for example, that our economy most needs "versatilists," people who have expertise in some domain *and* technology.[13] And in a much-cited book, *The New Division of Labor: How Computers Are Creating the New Job Market*, Frank Levy and Richard Murname (2004), an economist and educator coauthor team, analyze how computers are now carrying out the "rules-based part of jobs" so that skilled people can focus on the nonroutine parts. This means that well-paid, interesting, and nonroutine jobs will require a new type of expert thinking—that is, "the ability to bring facts and relationships to bear in problem-solving, the ability to judge when one problem-solving strategy is not working and another should be tried, and the ability to engage in complex communication with others" (6).

For an increasing number of jobs in the new economy, then, the cognitive bar has been raised, requiring a firm understanding of the problem-solving processes. And as Levy and Murname note, the line that marks the "digital divide" keeps shifting. In the 1980s when people spoke about the digital "haves" and "have-nots," it was about who knew how to use a keyboard and a mouse. By the 1990s, it was who knew how to use the Internet. Now, the economic and career landscape is completely transformed, and intellectual capabilities including "engaging in sustained reasoning, managing complexity, testing a solution" are all key (43).

But it is not just the economic landscape that is changing. The technological world is reshaping culture and political participation (Chadwick 2006). Issues and events that have profound consequences for the way we live our lives (from the creation of jobs, to scientific discovery, to fair voting procedures, to communication networks) are all being reshaped by technological knowledge. Who has this knowledge and who does not is consequential for democracy. What John Dewey (1916) said almost a century ago is still true today: education will only prepare people for life in a democracy when the educational experience is also democratic.[14] Unfortunately, *Stuck in the Shallow End* reveals how undemocratic our educational system still is in this technology age.

## Our Study

Our study was sparked in 1999 when Jane Margolis, along with Allan Fisher, then Carnegie Mellon's associate dean of computer science undergraduate education, was conducting research at Carnegie Mellon on the gender gap in computer science. The research findings and resulting interventions, described in *Unlocking the Clubhouse: Women in Computing* (Margolis and Fisher 2002), had significant impact on increasing the numbers of females enrolled in Carnegie Mellon University's computer science program. Yet during the years of this study (1994–1999), the numbers of African Americans and Latino/as majoring in computer science (at Carnegie Mellon University and nationwide) remained extremely low (Margolis and Fisher 2002). Margolis committed her next research project to understanding what was happening at the high school level for students of color. It is during high school when students make academic decisions that have the most serious implications for their college and/or career opportunities.

In 2000, Margolis was awarded an NSF grant, and our project, titled "Out of the Loop: Why Are So Few Underrepresented Minority High School Students Learning Computer Science?" began. Our team was built, and over a three-year period we immersed ourselves in three Los Angeles high schools. We made regular schools visits, conducted formal and informal observations, and interviewed educators and 185 students in these three schools. Our research sites were chosen based on their student demographics as well as their stated emphases and organizational philosophies. We picked schools that we thought would best offer a window into why students of color do—or do not—study computer science. To that end, we studied the courses offered, the quality of teachers, and the numbers and demographics of students who were enrolled in computer science courses within their schools as well as students' decisions to enter or exit (or their placement in) this computer science pipeline. We compared what we found to the national statistics and story. We focused on the experiences of the largest groups of students who are traditionally underrepresented in the field and who populate Los Angeles schools—African Americans, Latino/as, and females.[15] While our research investigated both the race *and* gender divide in computer science, our analysis and attention for this book is on the issues of race and social class. Although there is significant overlap between these issues, each is complex and deserving of undivided, careful attention. Still, previous and ongoing research on gender greatly informs our thinking in this book, and what we have learned from this study about race and class also informs thinking about gender. This book nevertheless focuses on our findings around the issue of race.[16]

In three extremely different schools, we asked students who were in computing or higher-level mathematics classes about their home and school computing experiences, their thoughts about computing and their future, how they decided about studying computer science (or not), their image of computer science, what interests them (and what does not), and why they think the field is so segregated. We asked educators and administrators about the computer offerings at the school, what type of students they think would be successful in computer science, the importance they place on learning computer science, and why they think the field is so segregated. We also talked with district administrators about the curriculum being offered. And we conducted regular informal observations of classrooms, labs, and after-school activities during our frequent school visits. The information we gleaned from these observations enabled us to provide the necessary context for analyzing our interviews.

Our study was focused on the traditional computer science sequence of courses. We know that currently there are innovative schools that are attempting to integrate the problem solving of computer science throughout the curriculum.[17] At the time of our study, this type of instruction was not present in the three schools we researched, and did not exist in most of the Los Angeles Unified School District (LAUSD) schools, so our focus remained on the traditional computer science sequence of classes.

## The District Context of the Three Schools

The three schools in our study are part of the larger LAUSD. The LAUSD is the second-largest school district in the country and one of the most diverse. It serves almost three-quarters of a million students. Nearly 75 percent of these students are Latino/a, with the next two largest groups being African American (11 percent) and whites (8 percent). Sixty-two percent of these students qualify for free and reduced-cost lunches.[18] This is a school district in great turmoil. Only 49 percent of ninth graders originally part of the class of 2004 went on to graduate, and only 18 percent of these ninth graders graduated with the requirements met to enroll in a four-year college or university. The district includes schools that "shock the conscience," a descriptor used in a lawsuit brought on behalf of students arguing that California's educational system is failing to meet its constitutional obligation to educate all students and educate them equally.[19] This lawsuit contends that there is a "constitutional floor below which no child's education should fall," and that low-income African American and Latino/a students disproportionately attend "substandard" schools.

The three schools we chose as our research sites typify other schools in the LAUSD, and yet differ greatly in their demographics. And in spite of the fact that they are all located in the same school district and share the same status as "digital high schools," it became clear that the learning opportunities differ according to the race and socioeconomic status of the school population.[20] Our research investigates why these disparities exist, how they unfold, and what the consequences are for the students in these schools.

Our research model focused on investigating the intricate interplay between school structures (in the form of course offerings, tracking patterns, counselor-to-student ratios, etc.) and belief systems, including psychological factors that could affect African American and Latino/a college-bound students' educational pathways (such as students' racial and identity issues in relationship to learning computer science, and teachers' assumptions and expectations for their students). This is a model of interaction that was derived from studies of school tracking and the disparities in mathematics and science learning across schools (Oakes 1989; Oakes and

Guiton 1995). We discuss more details about our data collection in appendix A of this book.

### Talking about Race

Talking and writing about race can be a sensitive and contentious issue, but it is always important. We are grateful for other researchers who have so finely articulated why, despite all the existing false notions that have been associated with distinct race categories, we must still proceed to examine "race," particularly when it comes to issues of inequality and education. While we insist that racial distinctions are *not* biologically valid and are instead the result of human-made lines drawn around different groups (Gould 1996; Pollock 2004), we also believe that racial distinctions matter because racial distinctions are prevalent in our society. In her new book *Can We Talk about Race?* Beverly Daniel Tatum, president of Spelman College, discusses using the language of race in our society: "Yet we still use the language of race, and need to, in order to describe what is taking place in the lives of particular groups of people, groups that have been socially defined on the basis of physical criteria, including skin color and facial features" (2007, xiv).

We are also deeply appreciative of the work by Harvard professor Mica Pollock (2004), who in her book *Colormute* examines how race is talked about, and not talked about, in schools. In an interview about her experiences interviewing students about race, she observes the following:

I saw young people in particular living out a very paradoxical treatment of race—this idea that race groups are not actually real but that people have made them real over time, so we have to deal with them. In my book on race talk, I boil this paradox down to the statement "we don't belong to simple race groups, and yet we do." Race groups are both not real and real simultaneously, and racialization is about walking that line. (Harvard Graduate School of Education 2002)

So in our book, one could say that we are walking that line. We refer to national or ethnic categories as racial, as do the students who Pollock found "were using these terms to negotiate in a system of power relations, a system of inequality, and I think that's why they called them racial—not because they thought they were biological" (ibid.). We agree with Pollock that race must be part of the conversation, because it is part of the *action*.

Our research on why so few African American and Latino/a high school students are learning computer science also concurs with Tatum's assertion that racial dynamics have prevented us from fully educating students of color. Throughout this research, we have witnessed how the low numbers of African American and Latino/a students studying computer science is commonly expected, reflecting the deeply entrenched stereotypes that plague our society. Just as African Americans are expected to be good basketball players, computer scientists are expected to be white or Asian males. Unfortunately, our culture is laden with these expectations, assumptions, and images. We turn on the television, switch to a channel of a basketball game, and without blinking an eye expect to see the court dominated by black male players. We switch to CNN to watch a board meeting of a major technology company or a young start-up in Silicon Valley, and do not blink an eye at the *lack* of African American, Latino/a, or female faces. These images of *who* belongs *where* lie deep within our psyche. Often, the way the world seems to "look," the segregation in these activities, is taken for granted and rarely questioned; the segregation seems normal, and as such, has become "normalized." We then consciously (but frequently unconsciously) assume that there is a "natural" and innate reason for this, that *these people are good at these things*—they have the knack, the skill, the mental propensity, and the inborn desire—and *those people are good at other things.*[21]

Our study challenges these assumptions and beliefs. Through our investigation of why so few African American and Latino/a students are learning computer science, we illuminate how seemingly different cultural preferences, abilities, and propensities that we see and assume about particular groups are deeply as well as directly connected to the inequality of access to meaningful opportunities across different fields and activities. We want to bring your eyes to these societal-level facts, which are often well hidden from view.

**Stuck in the Shallow End**

In chapter 1, we begin by explaining the central metaphor of our research. Through a summary of the tragic history of segregation in swimming, we set the stage for our account of what is going on in schools vis-à-vis computer science, and students' interest in and access to the topic. We then tell the research stories—the stories of computer science education at the three individual schools. These chapters reveal how students are afforded different, and highly unequal, computer science learning opportunities according to the racial and socioeconomic demographics of the students in the school. We found that schools often exacerbate inequalities in students' computing knowledge by systematically offering the most advanced course work to those students who already come from the most tech-savvy homes, while giving only the most basic course work to students with the least computing knowledge. Computer science then turns out to be a case study of the ways that the daily operations of schools become intertwined with the backgrounds of their students, and rather than being minimized or eliminated, "inequality is actually reinforced and exacerbated by the practices and biases of the school" (Noguera 2003, 74).

In chapter 2, we show how a school can be both technologically rich yet curriculum poor. We show how the simple provision of computers fails to address the absence of college-preparation and rigorous-learning opportunities. How the segregation in computer science becomes normalized to the point that it is simply taken for granted and uncontested is the focus of chapter 3. Then, by contrast, in chapter 4 we examine what happens in a so-called integrated school, in a white and wealthy neighborhood, that offers a full computer science pipeline of courses to its racially and ethnically diverse students; we examine how classes get segregated in this type of school, as we identify a process of "claiming" and ceding of spaces.

In *Stuck in the Shallow End*, we identify issues that go beyond computer science. We witness how students of color today are caught between Scylla and Charybdis.[22] In other words, as students of color navigate through schools such as the three different ones we have studied, there can be monsters on both sides of the channel. In low-resourced schools that are attended predominantly by minority students, students are faced with the poorest learning opportunities; in so-called integrated schools there may be more learning opportunities, but because of low expectations and other racially biased beliefs as well as behaviors, students of color are at psychological risk when entering these spaces. And in both of these situations, belief systems within the schools justify the segregation, making it seem natural, expected, and "just the way it is" to both students and teachers.

While we offer necessary critiques of how schools function, we do not regard the story we tell as a hunt for "bad guys." Rather, what we have found is that teachers and students are missing the necessary tools for change, and so our research instead indicts an educational system of interlocking inequalities that has been long in place and is difficult to dislodge. Yet despite the egregious reality we present in this book, we also tell a story of demonstrated possibility and transformation, and our final chapters have to do with changing the system.

The general problem of educational disparities, of poor-quality schools in communities where students are most in need of powerful educational opportunities, is rightly a multilayered, systemic, and national challenge. This challenge is created by broad patterns of residential segregation, residues of racism and bigotry, and ongoing socioeconomic disadvantage. We nonetheless believe that there are reforms that can be initiated today, on multiple levels, as we also work for a radical overhaul of our educational system. In our years of studying this problem, we have been impressed by the numbers of dedicated, committed, hardworking educators who are devoted to their teaching, schools, and students, and believe teachers are well positioned to bring about real change in the schools. As such, chapter 5 is about teachers as potential change agents.

We describe the actions our team took to intervene in the problems identified by our research. In collaboration with committed LAUSD leaders and teachers, within two years the number of AP computer science courses in the school district doubled, the number of Latino/as enrolled in AP computer science quadrupled, and the number of African Americans almost doubled.[23] On the surface, these results are remarkable, yet as anyone knows who has worked within public education, for every one step forward there are two steps back. *Stuck in the Shallow End* discusses these challenges, and how we are working to deepen and sustain these reforms.

In chapter 6, we describe a decade of educational policy about the digital divide, and show how national policy has missed the mark by focusing on "technology fixes" and not tying technology policy to broader social issues. We discuss how the No Child Left Behind legislation, which has nominally been designed to narrow the "achievement gap," has instead narrowed the curriculum and, in turn, the intellectual paths for students in low-performing schools. Our study of computer science is an exemplar of how current national educational policy is holding back the students that it claims it wants to advance. Our concluding remarks are followed by a methods appendix in which we reflect on the challenges of doing this type of research.

### One Point along the Pipeline

In the end, our book is an in-depth look at one point along the computer science "pipeline" from the perspective of what is occurring in three high schools in one urban school district. Our research thus does not speak about all schools, or even all schools in the LAUSD, but can nevertheless begin to open our eyes about these issues and suggest hypotheses for further study. But across these three schools, we have certainly learned that the image of a pipeline as a smooth and straight process is misleading. Borrowing the wonderfully descriptive words from *The Shape of the River*, a book that is "concerned about the flow of talent—particularly of talented black men and women—through the country's system of higher education and into the marketplace and the larger society," we have learned that "it is more helpful to think of the nurturing of talent as a process akin to moving down a winding river, with rock-strewn rapids and slow channels, muddy at times and clear at others.[24] Particularly when race is involved, there is nothing simple, smooth, or highly predictable about the education of young people" (Bowen and Bok 1998, xxi).

As we were finishing *Stuck in the Shallow End*, the U.S. Supreme Court handed down its ruling about school integration plans in Washington State and Kentucky.[25] Supreme Court Justice John Glover Roberts Jr., in the decision that struck down voluntary integration plans, argued that the "the way to stop discrimination on the basis of race is to stop discriminating on the basis of race." The story that we have uncovered about computer science education shows how deceptive this statement is. When working for school reform, failing to take race into consideration in fact perpetuates the segregation that still exists in the system. Many well-meaning people are at the center of determining *which* kids can learn *what*, and as a result, creating an unlevel playing field. But they are unaware of the role they or their schools are playing, or how their actions and beliefs—and the system within which they exercise them—are perpetuating a system of which they may not even approve.

*Stuck in the Shallow End* shows how segregation and inequality along racial lines operate on a daily basis in our schools, despite our best intentions and the denials now codified into law by the Supreme Court. They operate through the disparities in learning opportunities, the disparities in teacher quality, and the interplay between assumptions, stereotypes, and structural inequalities, all of which combine to make a noxious stew that preselects only certain students to be given the opportunities to move ahead in the twenty-first century. It operates through cultural assumptions that make inequality and segregation in computer science (and many other arenas) seem normal and natural. We write to show how this should not be, to make explicit how this all happens, and to make the invisible more visible.

# 1

## An Unlikely Metaphor: The Color Line in Swimming and Computer Science

What occurs in computer science education does not exist in isolation. As in other fields and activities where disparities in opportunities exist and are then rationalized, there are long-term consequences for both individuals and society. The history of segregation in swimming provides a powerful framework for these processes. It is, of course, possible to read *Stuck in the Shallow End* without this framework; the findings are just as relevant, the implications just as dire. But we believe that they enhance each other and that this separate yet connected story is one worth telling.

### The Shameful History of Swimming

The history of swimming, for communities of color, is a violent one. For African Americans, this history goes back to the events of Jim Crow and most likely to slavery. While the accounts of swimming during slavery are harder to pin down, there is near unanimity on what happened during Jim Crow and prior to the civil rights era, when access to swimming on beaches and in swimming pools was deeply segregated and off-limits to people of color.[1]

Historian Jeff Wiltse, author of *Contested Waters: A Social History of Swimming Pools in America*, writes about how violent this history has been. Wiltse's book opens with a description of the origins of public swimming pools in the late 1800s as bathhouses for the working poor (2007, 1). At that time, African American and white workers bathed together, with men and women bathing on alternate days. Yet approximately fifty years later at a swimming pool in Youngstown, Ohio, an incident depicted by Wiltse captures how dramatically things had changed. After winning the city baseball championship in 1951, a Little League team organized a celebration at a neighborhood pool. As the families and coaches of the team gathered to gain admittance to the pool party, all but one of the players was admitted—the one African American player, Al Bright. Wiltse reports how the other Little Leaguers swam in the water while Bright remained on the lawn outside the pool area. After a series of protests by the team and parents, Bright was allowed to come into the pool, but only after all the white swimmers had gotten out. Even then, while in the pool, the lifeguard forced Bright to sit inside a rubber raft. As Bright was escorted through the water on the raft, the lifeguard admonished him, "Whatever you do, don't touch the water" (2).

*Contested Waters* was written to investigate how it was possible that such a shift had occurred since the early bathhouse days, when African American and white swimmers coexisted in the water. The change came, in part, because in the early 1920s the utilitarian municipal bathhouses for the working poor were converted to leisure resorts. Following the transition, both genders and all classes swam together in these resorts, but people of color were not allowed entrance. When African Americans challenged the segregation by seeking admission to whites-only pools, there were violent white mob attacks on the African American swimmers. This happened not only in the South but also in many major northern cities.

Across the country, during the early 1900s, beaches as well as pools were sites of racist attacks against swimmers of color. In Chicago, in 1919, a violent race riot began after several African American teenagers who were swimming in Lake Michigan strayed into an exclusive area reserved for white swimmers. A gang of white bathers pelted them with stones, and one of the swimmers drowned. Crowds of African Americans gathered in protest, and seven days of rioting ensued (Wiltse 2007, 123; see also Pitts 2007). During the same time period, an all–African American resort in Manhattan Beach, California, was a refuge for minorities to visit the ocean without harassment. Owned and operated by the Bruce family, who were African American, the resort was attacked in the early 1920s by the Ku Klux Klan in an attempt to get the city to take back the land from the rightful owners. Under the pretense of building a city park, the city of Manhattan Beach did take the land away from the Bruce family, and African Americans were run off the land. It was not until 2007, practically eighty years later, that this travesty was acknowledged by the city and the beach was renamed Bruce's Beach (Schoch 2007). And photographs from the early 1940s in the Los Angeles Public Library show a two hundred foot roped-off stretch of the Santa Monica Beach that was established "for Negroes only" and called the "Inkwell."

Swimming segregation over numerous decades has had many different forms. In the South, Jim Crow laws kept African Americans out of the public swimming pools, and off the most desirable beaches and lakeside swimming spots. *Contested Waters* reports how in cities with a Southern heritage, such as Saint Louis and Washington, DC, the segregation of pools was official. In northern cities, segregation was de facto, encouraged by residential segregation. In the 1930s, Work Project Administration pools promoted swimming for all racial groups, but kept the swimming lessons separate. The pools were also mostly segregated in insidious ways such as the parks commissioner of New York City constructing the city's Work Project Administration pools in all-white communities. This meant that African Americans would have to enter the hostile white neighborhoods and consequently be at risk in the pools (Wiltse 2007, 140). In California, public pools were restricted to whites only, except on the day before the pool was drained and filled with clean water. A biography of Jackie Robinson describes how July 4, 1914, "symbolize(s) more vividly than any other the mean and divisive spirit of Jim Crow in Pasadena":

On that day, when city officials opened the sole municipal swimming pool, the Brookside Plunge in Brookside Park, they also restricted its use to Whites only. . . . After a storm of protest, the city instituted "International Day" at the pool—one day each week when anyone could use it. At the end of this day, they promised, the plunge would be drained and refilled with clean water. (Rampersad 1998, 21)

This "whites only" swimming policy affected *all* communities of color— Latino/as, Asians, and African Americans. As a history of Chicano school segregation reports (Montoya 2001), the plunge in Santa Ana, California, like the Brookside Plunge, had its "Mexican Day" on Mondays before the pool was cleaned. A children's book, *Sixteen Years in Sixteen Seconds* (Yoo 2005), tells the true story of Korean American diver Sammy Lee, who grew up in Los Angeles in the 1940s. Lee's dream was to become an Olympic diver, but like all the other kids of color, he was not allowed into the public pool except on "international day." On one of those special days, a coach noticed Lee practicing his dives and volunteered to be his coach. Because Lee could not get into the pool regularly but needed a place to practice, the coach dug a pit in his backyard and filled it with sand. So while white kids were learning to dive in the pool, Lee was diving into a pit of sand.

Throughout the northern United States around the mid-1950s, due to years of social and legal protests, municipal pools were finally desegregated, but this did not mean that African Americans and whites would now be swimming together (Wiltse 2007, 159). On the contrary, in response to desegregation orders, suddenly, starting in the middle of the 1950s, many whites began to abandon the municipal pools for private ones. The tension between whites and African Americans remained, however, and often there was violence around pool integration. Because of the explosive nature of these racist attacks, sparked by the hysteria around interracial intimacy in swimming, Wiltse explains how segregation in pools became a racial hot button and was viewed by some authorities as "more sensitive than schools" (156). And where violent attacks were not successful in shutting down the pools, other actions were taken. For example, in Mississippi, residents of the town of Stonewall buried the local pool in the 1970s rather than integrate (Nossiter 2006).

In low-income communities with high numbers of people of color, many of these municipal pools that were now open to everyone were not effective recreation centers for adults or teens (Wiltse 2007, 188). They were often "mini-pools"—concrete blocks surrounded by a chain-link fence (as opposed to the more parklike environment of the white-area pools)—that were typically so crowded that real swimming was practically impossible.[2] In any case, while the municipal pools flourished in the 1960s, by the 1970s the fiscal crisis in the cities brought about the deterioration and eventual closing of many of the pools (190).

The movie *Pride* (2007), situated in the mid-1960s, tells the true story of an all–African American swim team whose members began swimming in one of these abandoned centers. The film follows the devoted swim coach, Jim Ellis, as he literally cleans the pool (which had become a storage area, full of junk) and fills it with water, recruits a team of untrained swimmers, and holds the team together in the face of vicious racist attacks from the opposing all-white teams. The movie is ultimately about the phenomenal determination and bravery of the entire African American "PDR" team and Ellis.[3]

Lee and the PDR team are examples of extraordinary accomplishment against the odds. Lee went on to victory, winning an Olympic medal at the 1948 games. The PDR team won a tournament. They were determined and talented individuals, but they were also fortunate in that a coach found them, mentored them, gave them a place to practice, and helped them pursue a dream, despite all the bigotry and obstacles. And they are exceptions—for every Lee and PDR, there are generations of talented and determined kids who are literally chased out of the water. Whether the segregation was explicit or indirect, the end result has been the same: the history of swimming in this country is generations of people of color being denied access to adequate and safe swimming areas, being denied opportunities to learn to swim (Pitts 2007).[4] The current Centers for Disease Control drowning statistics, showing that African American youths drown almost three times more than white youths do, are all part of this horrendous historical legacy.[5]

## The Legacy Continues: Unequal Resources and Biased Beliefs

We have painted a historical portrait, but what is the situation now? Access to swimming opportunities is still separate and unequal. While the segregation during Jim Crow was legal and explicit, after the passage of the civil rights legislation, racial segregation still persists, but now in a more implicit fashion. In the late 1960s and early 1970s, the PDR team practiced in a decrepit facility, the only one available in their African American community at that time, yet the same shortage of quality resources is shockingly present today. In low-resourced communities with high numbers of families of color there are dramatically fewer year-round, accessible, quality swimming pools (DeGregory 2001; Glionna 2006; Shelburne 2007). In public schools (particularly lower-resourced, urban schools), physical education budgets are being slashed by as much as half, and costly aquatics programs often are the first to go (Aquatics International 2005). Swimming can also be an expensive sport, requiring access to a good year-round pool and a coach. Lessons are expensive too, and if a child goes on to become a competitive swimmer, the USA Swimming organization estimates participation in the sport could cost more than $1,000 to $2,000 per year (Slear 2002; Zinser 2006).

A recent *LA Daily News* article (Shelburne 2007) reports on Kristian Keith, a South Los Angeles teenager, who has a goal of making it to the U.S. Olympic swim team.[6] Keith trains at a local park pool, because neither the local high school nor the charter school she attends in Compton, a low-income African American area in Los Angeles, has a swim team or pool. In fact, of the eight schools in the LAUSD with the highest number of African American students, only one has a pool.[7] Yet as we write, across town in one of the whitest and wealthiest areas of Los Angeles, plans are being finalized for the construction of a $3.5 million aquatic center at a local charter high school. The center is being built to accommodate the city champion swim teams in Pacific Palisades, and a fundraising drive has been launched: a donor can gain naming rights to the competition pool for $500,000, the instructional pool for $350,000, the pool house for $300,000, the scoreboard for $150,000, and a swim lane for $50,000 each (Pascoe 2007).[8]

### Biased Beliefs: Blacks as Sinkers

In most cases of segregation, stereotypes and belief systems about different ethnic and gender groups' genetic make-up and physical abilities (and inabilities) emerge to rationalize unequal access and resulting disparities (Gould, 1996), and swimming is no exception. For instance, studies of the relatively minor differences in bone density between ethnic groups have been cited in explanations for the scarcity of black competitive swimmers (Entine 2000, 283).[9] The consequent rationale that African Americans do not swim because their bodies are not constituted for the sport quietly circulated for many years, and hit the big time in 1987 when Los Angeles Dodgers vice president Al Campanis, on the fortieth anniversary of Jackie Robinson's arrival into major league baseball, was a guest on Nightline with Ted Koppel. While Campanis was discussing his views on why there are so few African Americans in baseball management positions—specifically saying, "They may not have some of the necessities to be a field manager or perhaps a general manager" (cited in Wilhelm 1987)—he also went on argue that African Americans were not adapted to be swimmers because they are less buoyant. Although Campanis was fired from his position within forty-eight hours, his assertion was nevertheless indicative of biased assumptions with far-reaching implications.

Ironically, Campanis had a wide reputation for "fairness." Baseball's first African American manager, Frank Robinson, is reported as describing Campanis as a decent person who was simply a product of traditional thinking within the sports world. Robinson summarized this "traditional" view as: "Blacks aren't smart enough to be managers or third-base coaches or part of the front office. There's a belief that they're fine when it comes to the physical part of the game, but if it involves brains they just can't handle it" (cited in Wilhelm 1987).

Today, beliefs about African Americans' physical makeup and buoyancy problems are still present in the "common lore" about the racial gap in swimming. The USA Swimming organization, which has recently launched a nationwide diversity campaign, reports that these beliefs about African American "sinkers" have been passed from generation to generation, and are often internalized by children and adults (Slear 2002). This was on display at the Los Angeles Coliseum on June 30, 1990, at the celebration of Nelson Mandela's release from prison. Here, the late African American comedian Nell Carter hit a familiar place, joking before seventy thousand spectators (most of whom were African American) that swimming was "un-black"—for if they knew how to swim, there would be no African Americans, because all of their slave ancestors would have escaped back to Africa (cited in Dawson 2006, 26).

The accumulation of a violent history, denied access, and common lore beliefs has contributed to a greater fear of the water among African American adults. According to the Centers for Disease Control references, this fear and limited swimming ability has been more prevalent among African American women than among other demographic groups.[10] Those who are actively engaged in the campaign to diversify competitive swimming speculate that this fear has been handed down to each generation, certainly through the civil rights era (Ford 2006).[11]

## The Unlikely Comparison with Computer Science

Considering the dramatically different nature and histories of these two activities, how do we begin to compare the segregation in swimming with the underrepresentation in computer science? The answer lies in the fact that although at first glance they may seem quite different, the two endeavors share many qualities, from powerful historical legacies to inequitable trends rooted in false assumptions and beliefs.

Just as swimming is a "white sport" with a severe underrepresentation of swimmers of color, computer science is a world that is associated with a narrow stratum of our population: at any technology fair, those in attendance, hovering around the latest gadgets or crowding around the newest video games, are likely to be white and Asian males. It is also a world riddled with assumptions and explanations about who does well: "boy wonders" who have gravitated toward computing since they were young, magnetically attracted to machines all through adolescence, brimming over with the "natural" talent that makes them "whiz" kids, part of "the best and the brightest" (Margolis and Fisher 2002).[12] And because computers are presumed to be omnipresent—so anyone with an inclination would naturally be pursuing the field—people then conclude that the absence of African Americans, Latinos, and females within the field is a matter of "choice," interest, or talent.

This is where the segregation in swimming has been so instructive for us. In our society, African Americans are associated with excellent athletic abilities and physical dominance, and so their absence in swimming turns everything on its head. As recently as 2006, less than 1 percent of the 280,000-member USA Swimming organization was African American, and even fewer were Latino/a. The first African American male swimmer on the U.S. Olympic team was not until 2000; the first African American female swimmer was not until 2004. Cullen Jones, a young African American male swimmer, is expected to be the only new African American to compete in the Beijing Olympics in 2008. Considering our country's assumptions about African American physical talent, their effective absence from swimming should make no sense, and yet because of deeply held stereotypes and biases, and because the "whiteness" of the sport is so pervasive, it goes largely unquestioned. The race gap in swimming is the result not of any lack of "innate" talent or ability but rather institutional inequities and belief systems that have emerged to justify them. Therefore, while the histories of swimming and computer science are so different, while swimming is a physical activity and computer science is highly cognitive, there are many parallels between these two different worlds, and our own research reveals even more.

In swimming we see how the interplay between the inequality of structure, opportunities, and belief systems has resulted in a dramatic race gap in swimming; it is this same type of interplay that frames our understanding of the underrepresentation in computer science. In the next three chapters, we describe our research and show how low-resourced schools with high numbers of students of color are like the overcrowded, underdeveloped, shallow mini-pools. We reveal how opportunities to learn computer science in these schools are constricted and substandard, resulting in students being denied access to quality learning opportunities and thereby being stuck in the shallow end. We show how widespread belief systems within the schools justify these less powerful learning experiences by regarding students of color as "not interested" or "not capable" of handling the material. Just as swimming has become identified as a white "country club" sport, the field of computer science has become identified with a narrow stratum of the population: white and Asian males. Both swimming and computer science have a similar challenge before them. Both must increase access to quality learning opportunities, challenge belief systems that mask and rationalize the inequities, and change a culture that assumes that students of color belong in the shallow end.

## Preferences and "Personal Choice"

USA Swimming, the national organization of swim teams, has recently embarked on a major outreach campaign to diversify competitive swimming. It is also working to ensure that swimming lessons are available for kids in underserved communities. National organizations such as Make a Splash along with local initiatives through groups like the Boys and Girls Clubs of America have emerged all over the country.[13] But USA Swimming has found that in addition to initiating efforts to increase access, a campaign is needed to confront today's "cultural disconnect" between swimming and the African American community, and it has undertaken this task (Pitts 2007). Not only does swimming have a reputation as a "country-club sport," belonging to swimmers from middle-class white families that have access to the finest year-round facilities, but coaches are having to fight against the notion that "blacks don't swim" and "swimming is uncool." Again, their uphill battle mirrors the one in computer science.

As we said in our introduction, we could not walk away from what we learned about swimming. Our thinking would never be the same after we began to investigate why it was that African American children were drowning at a rate higher than white children. Learning what we did propelled us into writing this book, and became the way we felt we could communicate what we were witnessing in the schools. What we have learned about swimming and computer science is that all of the seemingly cultural preferences and interests are profoundly impacted by historical legacies, structural inequities, denied learning opportunities, and belief systems that justify these inequities. We hope that our comparison of these two extremely different activities can help us all become more acutely aware of how the violent racist past still lives on today in almost every aspect of our lives—from the tragic loss of lives due to drowning, to the sports we play, to the knowledge we do or do not acquire.

# 2

# Technology Rich, But Curriculum Poor

East River High School, the first of our three case studies, is a critically overcrowded school in East Los Angeles, with nearly five thousand students—almost all Latino/a—filling its hallways.[1] In what turned out to be one of many contradictions at East River, the school is teeming with computers, and yet significant computer science learning opportunities for its students are few and far between. As we spent time on this campus, we began to see the daily structural realities that contribute to the low numbers of students of color learning computer science. Indeed, at East River the structural challenges and organizational complexities were dense, thorny, and at times impenetrable. We gained an understanding of how these complex institutional issues interact with personal belief systems, and in the pages that follow, we examine this interplay, showing how it results in extremely shallow curricula, with students being exposed to little beyond the most elementary computing skills. For the thousands of students who must contend with them, these limited offerings have significant implications in terms of not only computer science but also education more generally.

## East River High School

East River High School is located in an East Los Angeles neighborhood not far from the industrial complexes that dominate the area. Several freeways cross into the community boundaries to access these businesses, contributing to the high level of air pollution that hangs over the campus. Built for fifteen hundred, East River currently has close to five thousand students. The school is bursting at the seams, and to make room for its enormous student population, East River operates year-round with three different "tracks" of students, each following a different calendar. The school is classified by the state of California as "critically overcrowded" because it enrolls almost three times more students per acre than is considered acceptable by state standards. Although the hallways are nearly empty during class time, the moment the bell rings, students fill the space shoulder to shoulder while trying to navigate through the crowd to get to their next classes.

This is a school that has experienced phenomenal transitions over the last forty years. In 1969, out of forty-seven high schools in the LAUSD, East River had the smallest student enrollment. Of the 1,642 students at the time, 21 percent were classified as "white/Spanish surname," and 76 percent as "white/other white." Yet over the past five decades, the demographics of the East River community have shifted dramatically. With a rapidly growing local population, the number of students at East River High School has almost tripled in less than four decades, representing the largest enrollment increase in any LAUSD senior high school in history.

East River High School serves students living in its surrounding community, 99 percent of whom are Latino/a. There is a great deal of heterogeneity in this almost-exclusively Latino/a community: over half the population is foreign born, with families coming from many different countries of origin, including Mexico, El Salvador, Guatemala, Honduras, and other Latin American nations. Thirty-five percent of the students at East River are English-language learners, and based on family income levels, 93 percent of the students qualify for free or reduced-cost lunches. The parents of only 13 percent of the students at East River have attended some college, and a mere 9 percent have college degrees.[2] East River typifies many schools with high Latino/a populations—more than other ethnic groups, Latino/as are likely to attend schools that are segregated on the basis of race and class, and are concentrated in schools with high poverty levels (Orfield and Lee 2005).

After scoring in the lowest decile statewide on California's Academic Performance Index, East River has been labeled an underperforming school and put on notice by the state.[3] In spite of this (or perhaps in part because of this), the daily operation of the school is like a well-oiled machine assuring that all students and teachers (and visitors) are in the right place at the right time. A young security guard at the school's entrance asks visitors in Spanish or English to sign in. During the morning break and at lunchtime, the students quickly make their way to the outside courtyard to eat; administrators guard the doors, not allowing students into the hallways, computer labs, or interior classrooms without a

teacher's note. During lunch, the students spend much of their time waiting patiently in the cafeteria line. Military recruiters are sometimes found
on campus, lining the lunchtime plaza with their tables and literature. A
series of wall murals depicting Chicano history provides wonderful visual
relief throughout the schoolyard.

## The Glow of Technology Cannot Hide the Lack of Computer Science Curriculum

[East River] is an average school. It's just there's a lot of schools out there that
I know that are a lot better. I'm not saying this school's bad, but it's just that
there's a lot of schools out there that I know have better teachers, have better
schedules. . . . The whites and Asians make more money, and they could put their
children into better schooling.
—Marisa, intermediate algebra student

As we began our research in 2001, East River was considered a Digital
High School success story. The Digital High School legislation, enacted in
1997, provided $1 billion over four years to supply computers and Inter-
net access to California's high schools, and this provided a jump-start for
the school's technology program. By the 2004–5 school year, there was a
5.8:1 student to computer ratio—a high rate compared to the state average of 4.4:1. A school-produced video celebrates the technology at East
River, showing classroom after classroom filled with rows and rows of
translucent royal blue user-friendly computers, all installed and working
throughout the school—from the Internet publishing class, to the library,
to the photo labs, to the college counselor's office. Besides the equipment itself, the central stars of the video are the enthusiastic and devoted
teachers who worked tirelessly to supplement the Digital High School
funding in order to create and sustain this technology-rich environment.
For years, during school, after school, and on weekends, these teachers
volunteered their time to raise funds and carry forth their vision.

Over the last couple of years, the school has continued to pump up the
technology throughout the campus. A series of recent LAUSD promotional videos shows a variety of technology-laden pockets at East River:
a film-editing lab filled with new computers and film-editing software, a
technology-rich computer-aided design center, and a graphics arts class.
Each video features an enthusiastic teacher and eager students. East River
is understandably proud and excited about these classes that students
clearly enjoy.

For those concerned about providing access to technology for students of all socioeconomic backgrounds, this school's instructional network appears at first glance to be a glowing success story, showing how an under-resourced school situated in a low-income area, with all odds against it, could bridge the digital divide. But for our research team investigating why there are so few African American and Latino/a students learning computer *science* in high school, we watch the glossy, upbeat videos and are still left wondering, What is wrong with this picture?

At a time when policymakers were issuing alarms about the decline in the nation's computing and engineering talent, the only computer course that even meets college preparatory guidelines in California, AP computer science, has never been taught at East River. In the three years that we spent at the school (2001–3), the computer science curriculum was shrinking at a troubling pace: a programming course, the school's most advanced offering, was taught on only one track, and as such, was a choice available to only one-third of the East River students, and even that was canceled after only two years. In fact, ultimately, no East River computing class went beyond cut-and-paste instructions, and despite the glow of technology, there were no classes that introduced the problem solving and scientific reasoning of computer science to allow students to more fully understand all that the field has to offer. And so what provided the most disturbing disconnect between the videos and what we observed at East River was that despite this "technologically rich" portrait, the computer *science* curriculum available to East River students was paltry. In fact, by the second year of our research, it could best be described as nonexistent.[4]

## A Short-lived Course: The Story of the Programming Class

At East River, computer programming was offered during our first two years of data collection (2001–2 and 2002–3). We observed this course over both years, as it was the most advanced computer science offering in the school. (The other two courses in the department focused on literacy and application skills.) The dedicated instructor for the programming class, Mr. McGrath, was a mathematics teacher who volunteered to teach the class because of his long-held interest in programming. He had received no formal training in the subject, but taught himself at home on an archaic TRS-80 computer.

By district standards, the programming class had a small enrollment in the two years we conducted observations. During the 2001–2 academic year, there were twenty students in the class, split evenly by gender. The boys in the class were older, mostly juniors and seniors who were the "techies" of the school, the ones most interested in technology, sparked largely by video games and, in many cases, their social networks outside of school. For instance, Fernando, a twelfth grader, was considered by the teacher and his classmates to be the most knowledgeable programming student. He became interested in computing through a male friend of his, outside of school, who taught him how to build and host Web sites for extra money—an endeavor that served as a part-time job for Fernando throughout high school. In an example of the importance of social networks in sparking and nurturing interest in computing (especially in the absence of engaging school instruction), Fernando recruited three of his male friends to the second year of the programming class.

There were two groups of girls in the class: one was a small group of tenth graders that McGrath specifically recruited from his mathematics class because he thought they would find it interesting; the other was a group of girls, also mostly sophomores, who described themselves as having been "dumped" into the class. "Dumped" is the term that students, teachers, and administrators use when students are placed into a class without requesting it. This happens often at East River because students might need the credits and a particular class is open, or because a class needs more students and the students have a free period.

In a typical class period, McGrath followed a textbook that the students did not have copies of. He based his instruction on transcribing programs from the book onto an overhead projector and occasionally explaining different aspects of programming, such as looping.[5] During his first year of teaching the class, he would stay a few days ahead of the students, learning the material as he went. The class time consisted of students sitting at their terminals while McGrath sat at his desk working on the same program the students were working on. When McGrath did offer a lesson for the class, students sat silently and copied the program he posted on the overhead projector. The students then sat at their computers and typed in that same program.

Instead of teaching programming as a problem-solving skill, in a context that these East River students would likely find challenging, engaging, and meaningful, the assignments throughout the year were typically input-output problems that did not come close to utilizing the critical thinking skills of computer science. For example, one assignment asked students to write a program that when given the dimensions of several rooms in a house, would compute the cost of carpeting the home. This is a problem that uses middle school mathematics skills at best, and could have easily been solved using a calculator. Other assignments focused on basic trivia games, including a hangman game, a state capital game, a tic-tac-toe game, and a program that provides a test for students studying the area of basic geometric figures. None of these assignments featured the problem solving and scientific reasoning that is the foundational knowledge of computer science; none capitalized on the high-level processing power that is central to the field of computer science; and none situated it in real-world scenarios that emphasized the wide applicability of computer science expertise.

This is not a singular indictment of McGrath for he was a dedicated teacher who volunteered to teach this class, believing it was important that this subject be available for East River students. Rather, the pedagogy he employed typifies how programming is commonly presented at the high school level—disengaging and isolated from the problem solving and scientific reasoning that is at the core of computer science. [6]

Students' reactions to the class were mixed, with the most common complaint being boredom. The small group of tech-savvy boys, some of whom were taking the class for the second time, felt that it was going slower than they wished, and that they were not learning enough. Eduardo, for example, called the class "too easy and childish," and his friend Jose noted that he was unable to progress at a satisfying pace because his classmates "ask lots of dumb stuff [that] they should know." The girls who had been recruited were happy they took the class despite some boredom. For instance, Vanessa explained that at first she did not enjoy the class because it was "different" from what she was used to, but then she "was like, 'oh, wow, this is cool!' And I liked it at the end." Vanessa did add that "it was still kind of boring," however. The girls who were dumped into the class (and therefore were the least likely to have had an outside interest in the topic) often felt lost, especially in comparison to their more knowledgeable, older, and male classmates who, as one student described, "talk down to us."

Despite our criticisms of the class, we were still concerned when it was canceled after two years, for it was the only course available at East River for students who wanted to go beyond basic word-processing or application skills and learn more about computer science. The elimination of the class was both shocking and disappointing to McGrath. Although he recognized that his teaching was hurt by his lack of subject expertise and acknowledged that he was learning as he went along, McGrath felt that he was becoming more proficient in programming and providing the students a unique opportunity that they would not get elsewhere. His initial assessment of why the class was suspended was budgetary cuts. We were aware of the budget constraints at East River, but we also noted how little support McGrath had for teaching this class. He lacked professional development instruction as well as a community of other computer science teachers to learn from. In short, straightforward budget issues seemed too simplistic of an explanation. So we asked ourselves, What factors contributed to the cancellation of the programming class? And what does the answer tell us about the shaping of the curriculum at schools like East River?

## Overcrowding and Multitrack Calendar

The pressure of running a critically overcrowded and underresourced system is felt in all aspects of academic life at East River. Making sure students have a full academic schedule that meets all their graduation needs is a logistical nightmare. Additionally, like many other over-crowded schools, East River has been tagged as a low-performing school, which means extreme scrutiny from the state, interventions, and threats of budget cuts and even closure—all distractions (necessary or not) from the day-to-day business of educating students.

In order to accommodate all the students in this overcrowded school, East River (as well as its feeder middle school) has been forced to operate on multiple tracks./ This means that students have fewer days of instruction each school year, with longer school days to meet the state instructional minutes requirement, and only two-thirds of the students are "on track" at any given time. Administrators, teachers, and students alike constantly struggle with this system—such as the complexity of scheduling classes; teachers not being able to have their own classrooms; students returning after a two-month absence to take high-stakes stan-dardized tests; student attrition; and the inability of students to take sum-mer school classes or hold summer jobs. For example, one student we spoke with, Mario, explained the toll this system takes on his grades: "I think I have testing after 'vacation,' so it's like . . . I don't remember how to do anything. That's the bad thing about this track: two months off, then come back and test." The constant and overwhelming effort re-quired to accommodate almost five thousand students on changing tracks takes priority over other concerns, especially when it comes to classes like computer science that are often viewed as luxuries in daily school operations.

When we talked with the assistant principal of counseling at East River, Mr. Walton, about the computer science offerings, he described the constraints of the master schedule, and how balancing class size is essential to keeping the school running. East River's multitrack calendar makes it significantly more difficult to enroll students in specialized classes, and the programming course also cost money that the school needed to channel elsewhere, specifically in areas such as mathematics and language arts that are subject to state tests. As Walton explained to us, "We lay out our matrix. . . . We only have so much time on the master schedule. We only have so many cells here on this schedule and we're only allowed so many teachers. If I opened up the programming class that means that . . . OK, so one less mathematics class." So because McGrath is a mathematics teacher, if he teaches a nonmathematics class such as programming, this leaves a hole in the mathematics schedule and it costs money to have another teacher cover that period. Further, because programming had a relatively low enrollment, it was not seen as a cost-effective way to use a mathematics teacher. These trade-offs typify the constant triage decision making that afflicts large, overcrowded, low-resourced schools (Oakes and Rogers 2006, 158–163). And while McGrath was correct that budget issues played a part in the cancellation of computerprogramming, financial constraints were compounded by a system that must constantly choose one thing over another in order to survive. The end result is that classes that are perceived to have more limited interest or utility, like computer programming, get canceled.

### Floristry Instead of Computer Science: The Lack of Student Supports and Guidance

Computer science in the Los Angeles schools is not part of the core curriculum and instead falls into the broad curricular category of technical arts. The classes are electives, and although each student must take a technical arts course to graduate, at East River their options include disparate choices such as floristry and child care. And while we have already talked about students being dumped into computer science courses, the reverse also happens. In other words, a student may be interested in programming, but because of overcrowding or scheduling conflicts, ends up in floristry instead, simply to keep that student moving toward graduation. This is exactly what happened to Suzanna:

*Interviewer:*   How did you get into the floristry class?

*Suzanna:*   'Cause it's a technical art. You need a [tech arts] class in order to graduate, and the computer class was [full], and there is no room for me.

*Interviewer:*   If you had a choice between floristry and another semester of programming, what would you choose?

*Suzanna:*   Programming. . . . I am not really a girly girl, so the flower thing is not really me.

*Interviewer:*   Did the counselor put you in that [floristry] class?

*Suzanna:*   Yeah, 'cause it was either that, or I would have taken service again.

Suzanna was a strong mathematics student who was interested in learning programming. We interviewed Suzanna in her precalculus class. That she, or any other student, is assigned to floristry without an express interest, or allowed to enroll in service (doing tasks such as running errands for the front office) sometimes multiple times instead of an academic class, is a sign of how derailed the college preparatory system is at schools like East River.

In spite of the potential that counselors have to be important gatekeepers and play critical roles in determining which courses students take, it is difficult to be surprised by the seeming indifference that Suzanna describes. East River has a 545:1 student-to-counselor ratio (California Department of Education 2004). As a result, quite a few students talked about having little interaction with their counselors; in some cases, they felt their counselors did not have time to meet with them at all. Gabriela, for example, explained, "I don't like my counselor . . . he's like, 'Oh, leave me alone, I'm out of here,' or 'Wait until I'm at the office or schedule a date for me to call you up or something.'" While this instance may be equally indicative of the counselor's personal style and the staggering caseload he is contending with, it nevertheless speaks clearly to the fact that with scarce resources, the responsibility of creating class schedules for almost five thousand students on three different academic tracks is an overwhelming component of counselors' jobs. Ensuring that courses are "balanced" and fiscally feasible is an ongoing struggle that consumes an enormous portion of the counselors' time and energy, as does the push for them to focus more attention on issues like dropout prevention and discipline (Lombana 1985; McDonough 2004; Monson and Brown 1985). This leaves precious little time for exploring particular courses of study like computer science that may or not be fully understood by counselors or students. In many cases, students reported, counselors simply assigned them to classes without discussing any future educational options. Given its poor positioning within the overall curriculum, it is not surprising that computer science does not fare well in the process.

## The Power of Testing and Accountability Pressures

At East River, the largest force of state and district pressure is directed at raising scores on annual standardized tests. The pressure is immense; if test scores do not improve, the school administrators risk losing their jobs, and the school could face a state takeover. This places additional pressure on the school to focus on "the basics" and "teach to the test." "Extras"—subjects that do not help to improve standardized test scores, like art, music, and computer science—do not receive attention or resources, and are therefore subject to cuts and cancellation. As a result, many students in schools like East River are funneled into extra remedial mathematics and language arts classes in the hopes that this will help them score better on the tests, which are perceived by many to define the quality of the school. At the same time they are steered away from electives, courses that are seen as peripheral and less important.

As we sat with the East River principal, talking about the computer science curriculum and the cancellation of the computer programming class, he pointed to four large binders behind his desk containing the list of skills the students are required to master. Computer science was nowhere to be found; despite the role that it plays across multiple disciplines and arenas, it is not considered a core academic subject. One need only look at the district's computer literacy graduation requirements to understand the basic way that technology is conceived of at a policy level.[8] In order to graduate, a student must either take one of the computing-related courses offered in the schools, such as Internet publishing, or pass a computer literacy test that includes the following relatively rudimentary tasks:

- Save a document into your traveling folder
- Type, proofread, and correct sentences in a word-processing document
- Adjust margins, alignment, change type styles, adjust type size, use bold, italicize and underline, and so on

• Find information and images on the Internet, and copy them into a word-processing document

And so when it comes to technology, we see the same effect of testing pressures, but in reverse. Any attempts to teach to the test of technology competency will automatically concentrate on this basic level.

Testing largely defines the curriculum at East River, as it does at other schools in similar situations, as educators are forced to focus the balance of their resources toward raising scores on federally mandated No Child Left Behind tests and increasing the passing rates of students on the newly developed California High School Exit Exam.[9] Because of all the testing pressures being juggled in the school, none of which include computer science, the principal said that the only way he could have kept programming on the schedule was if he could have shown that student achievement, based on standardized test scores, was improving because of the class. But in actuality, test scores had been declining over the previous two years. As we walked down the school's hallways, we could feel the testing frenzy, as all the walls were covered in large colorful posters of sample exam questions and answers, offering further evidence that the focus on federal and state mandates—and their arsenal of prescribed assessments—falls heaviest on schools that perform the poorest on testing measures.

**Carefully Follow Directions: The Effects of Belief Systems**

According to the Association of Computing Machinery, the nation's computer science professional organization, an exemplary K–12 computer science curriculum should, among other things, prepare students to understand the nature of the discipline and its place in the modern world, help them to recognize it as a field that interleaves principles and skills, and equip them to use computer science skills (especially algorithmic thinking) in problem-solving activities in other subjects. The association recommends a sequence of four computer science courses to gradually build on these interdisciplinary principles and competencies (Tucker et al. 2004). Though these goals may seem lofty in light of other school priorities, these recommendations point out the deeper principles underlying the surface manifestations of computing. Sadly, the curriculum at East River, with a heavy vocational emphasis, does not come close to these standards, and the Internet publishing course at the school serves as a case in point.

Internet publishing was one of the classes with the largest enrollments at East River. Because it satisfies the yearlong technical arts graduation requirement, fifty students packed this classroom, five periods a day, during each track, to enroll in what was the most advanced computer class offered at East River. The setup of the classroom was custom designed by the two instructors, Mr. Blake and Mr. Sullivan, who each had worked at the school for over thirty years and were completely committed to every aspect of the course. The students' desks, each with its own computer, faced the front of the classroom, where the instructors' work areas peered down from a heightened platform. The instructors' computers were networked to control the students' computers. Occasionally, the teachers would interrupt diligently working students by freezing the class computers to teach a lesson, or a teacher would monitor an unknowing student across the classroom through his computer. A banner on the wall reminded students that the only rule was to "carefully follow directions."

Students worked independently from a prescripted curriculum designed by the instructors, following the directions in the online manual from lesson to lesson. They were not encouraged to collaborate; in fact, on many occasions we would watch one of the instructors chastise students for interacting with each other, even if their dialogue was related to the assignment. Class activities connected to publishing in a broad sense. As Blake explained, "We teach how to do drawing, business cards, how to use word processing, flyers, all kinds of handouts, newspaper publishing." A midsemester assignment, for example, required students to duplicate an advertisement from the yellow pages, and grades on this assignment were awarded based on the fidelity of their images.

Henry, a senior enrolled in the course, was one of the sixty East River students we interviewed for our study. He told us that he was interested in learning more about computer science to further his passion for cartooning and computer animation, and as he showed us his notebooks of drawings, Henry explained that he had enrolled in the Internet publishing class for two consecutive years. He was enthusiastic about ultimately creating his own Web page, and in this class he now worked without much guidance. Using the indicators that he considered important, Henry said he believed this course had helped him work toward his academic and career goals in digital animation. In a conversation with a member of our research team about how he thought he had benefited from taking the same noncollege credit course for two years in a row, Henry focused on typing skills:

*Interviewer:* Do you feel like you're moving up, learning more every year?

*Henry:* Yeah, I'm pretty much faster now.

*Interviewer:* What do you mean [by] "faster"?

*Henry:* I used to type, like, forty [words] per minute. My basic typing skills went up.

In an eerie echo of the findings of a previous study that showed affluent schools use computers to teach higher-order thinking skills while poorer schools use them for "drill and kill" (Warschauer 2000), Henry's Internet publishing course has spent almost two years teaching him elementary desktop publishing skills. Not until the end of the second year was Henry introduced to Web page design, and even then Web publishing was not part of the curriculum. Henry knows what he has been taught. He does not yet know how much he has not been taught.

Considering the online interests of students, this course could have easily served as a compelling "hook" into learning more about the fundamental concepts of computer *science*, such as the notion of formal languages that are interpretable by computers and the multitier architectures that underlie Internet applications, but unfortunately this did not happen. Instead, the course focused on low-level skills, touching on few basic principles of computer science, and rote memorization. And regrettably for East River students interested in pursuing a computer-related field, this was the most advanced course offered at the school.

### Deficit Belief Systems Interact with School Structures

At East River, it is undeniable that structural constraints such as the size of the school, overcrowded conditions, teachers' qualifications, funding limitations, and accountability and testing pressures dramatically impact the curricula. But the beliefs within the school walls also play a part. We quickly saw firsthand how belief systems both contribute to this constrained curriculum and frame how educators make sense of as well as justify schooling decisions (Oakes and Guiton 1995). Again, the East River Internet publishing class illustrates this point.

The two teachers of Internet publishing, Blake and Sullivan, as we noted earlier, both have been in the school for decades, and both have shaped this course and its curriculum over the last eighteen years. Blake discussed why he likes teaching at East River, explaining that the "school has good kids" and they are "fairly well behaved." Yet he was also quick to add that he believes his students arrive with limitations, citing his belief that "they don't have much interest in learning" and "have very little parent support toward education." Likewise, Sullivan also mentioned some of his students' backgrounds as diminishing their academic capacities and problem-solving abilities:

There are some students that just because of their background, they have never been able to—they don't know how to problem solve. . . . They're at a total loss. . . . They don't have that curiosity because they've been spoon-fed by their moms and dads all—their whole life. Given answers, given answers, given answers, and so they don't have that ability or desire to figure things out or explore. They just sit there and look at the screen: "Well, I don't know how to do it." They don't know! "Well, did you try?" "Well, no, 'cause nobody showed me." "Well, did you try to even look at it?" "No." And so we have a few kids like that.

So while Blake and Sullivan, both white teachers, clearly enjoy their students, talking about how they are well behaved and "love this stuff" (referring to technology), both teachers also articulated deficit-based views that are often heavily concentrated in schools with high numbers of Latino/a students: "they don't have much interest in learning," "they have little parental support," "they don't know how to problem solve," "they're at a total loss," "they don't have that curiosity," and "they don't have that ability or desire to figure things out or explore."[10] As a result, Blake and Sullivan have designed their "follow directions" class to match their expectations for their students.

How is it that two teachers who profess to love teaching their students so much can also knowingly design their course in such a basic, technical, elementary way? Two important issues—students' language acquisition and the historical roots of vocational education (which encompasses computer science)—shed light on this seeming contradiction.

At schools with large percentages of English-language learners, language issues are often cited as evidence that students are not ready or able to learn. East River was no exception. One of the most committed and dedicated educators at this school, Mr. Costa, blamed the failure of a school-business technology training partnership that East River attempted on this very issue:

I mean, we get kids coming into high school here who are reading at the third- and second-grade levels. And, for example, we tried to start and we have started a Cisco Networking Academy here, but the students don't do particularly well because they have a reading level in general that's not sufficient to handle the online materials that are part of the course.

It is true that concentrations of English-language learners provide a real challenge for schools and the district at large. Currently, English-language learners make up 25 percent of the public school population, and too many are faring badly in the schools (Callahan 2005). Over a decade of research has shown how English learners are particularly inadequately served in California secondary schools, especially with respect to college preparation:

[Their] lack of preparation for higher education results not so much from their limited English skills, although there is an indirect correlation, as from inherent barriers in the structure of their schooling; poorly trained teachers, a mismatch between the academic literacy needs of [English learners] and the didactic nature of most language learning environments, low track placement, insufficient time to achieve their academic goals, and perhaps most importantly, the absence of any clear focus on postsecondary opportunities for them. (Callahan and Gándara 2004, 9)[11]

In a study of technology use in eight California high schools (in both low- and high-socioeconomic neighborhoods), researchers reported one administrator in a low-socioeconomic-status (SES) school describing a de facto two-track system: the academic "university" track and the survival/vocational "California track" for the English learners (Warschauer, Knobel, and Stone 2004). The researchers described this latter track as "aimed at equipping large numbers of immigrant students, who enter secondary school with little knowledge of English and limited reading and writing skills in any language, with operational understandings that will, at the very least, help them get by in California as adults" (586).

This line of thinking is hardly new. It has its roots in the history of vocational education, and as noted earlier, computer science currently falls under this umbrella. The vocational tradition is one in which "hand" work has been considered separate from (and less than) "brain" work, and in which certain kids are prejudged as not being capable of or needing the brain work. Historically, students who have been excluded from the brain work are students of color and recent immigrants—a trend that can be traced to the end of the nineteenth and start of the twentieth centuries, when the emerging science of IQ testing, premised on widespread beliefs about the different potential abilities of different social and ethnic groups, coincided with a growing need for factory workers. The result was a legitimization of compulsory schooling that prepared different groups of students for separate life paths—vocational or professional work.[12] As Lewis Terman (1923, 28), the intelligence-testing pioneer, long ago wrote about immigrants, Mexicans, and blacks: "Their dullness seems to be racial. . . . Children of this group should be segregated in special classes. . . . [T]hey cannot master abstractions, but they can often be made efficient workers."

And while it would never be voiced in such terms today, the legacy persists. Mike Rose (2005), in his recent book *The Mind at Work*, explores this brain/hand dichotomy, including in the context of vocational education. In a survey of the past thirty years of academic journals on the topic, he reports finding few articles addressing the intellectual aspects of this type of learning. In the few instances where they were covered, "they tended to have a remedial focus, or they were a response to policy directives from outside the profession" (177). In spite of the fact, as Rose demonstrates in this book, that much work involving the hands clearly requires higher-order thinking, the academic caliber of vocational education simply has not been a concern, and the academic potential of students in these courses simply has not been explored, whether because of a reliance on faulty "intelligence" measures or erroneous assumptions about the effects of being an English-language learner.

The lasting effects of low expectations, a lack of access to rigorous courses, and de facto tracking practices are that African American and Latino/a students are far more likely to be judged as having learning deficits, and to be placed disproportionately in low-track remedial programs where they have less access to high-status knowledge, powerful learning environments, and resources (University of California Accord 2006).[13] And the irony, of course, is that even though computer science is classified as vocational education by East River educators, there nevertheless remains a more rigorous upper echelon—the AP computer science courses—that is inaccessible to the students of color that vocational education was originally designed to serve.[14]

## High Hopes with Low Opportunities

As we investigated the computer science learning opportunities at East River, it was the conversations with the students that most broke our hearts. We heard how so many of them were not being given adequate guidance or assistance in planning for their futures, were taking service classes multiple times instead of academic courses, did not have comparable learning opportunities to their counterparts in schools with white and more wealthy students (as we will discuss in chapter 4), and did not realize how they were being shortchanged. Even those students who expressed an interest in technology had little understanding about the field of computer science, the courses they should be taking, or what they should be learning beyond basic computing skills. Nevertheless, they were aware that they were not being afforded the same opportunities as their peers in more resourced schools. Vanessa, a student at East River, explained her perspective: "Well, because at the Hispanic schools . . . classes are really not that offered. . . . You hardly know that there are classes. Like, if I would have known there are computer classes, I would have gone to it, but they don't say anything."

Other students who have found the computer classes appear not to be benefiting from them in the ways that one would hope. We have already introduced Henry, a student in the Internet publishing course who was lacking both the knowledge and broader understanding that would equip him to continue a course of study in computer science. Another student, Christina, a senior, planned to attend California State University at Long Beach after graduation to study computer science. She was a strong mathematics student, and the first one in her family to think about pursuing computer science in college. While we were talking with her about why she thought she would be good at computer science, Christina told us: "I'm the one who uses the computer the most out of my home, and I'm the one who's always, like, trying to fix it or trying to work with it." After telling her counselor about her interest, her counselor placed her in the basic introduction to computers class. Christina was not aware of any other computer courses in the school, but told us that she would unquestionably take additional classes if she knew they were offered. Her counselor, though, had never mentioned any other classes, and Christina's understanding of the field was elementary at best.

With only the introductory course under her belt, Christina also referred to her computer class as the "typing class." Christina went on to tell us that she wished her school would provide instruction beyond the basics of word processing, Microsoft Excel, and PowerPoint, though she felt confident that she would be able to take more advanced courses and "catch up" in college as part of her computer science major. Unfortunately, we know from other studies that students who arrive at college with inadequate preparation face significant struggles as they attempt to catch up to their peers. A review of California State University's placement tests found that a disproportionate percentage of students from low-performing schools like East River (students who are typically Latino/a or African American) are placed into remedial classes when they arrive at college, further highlighting the lasting impact of this lower-level curriculum. The California State University system's Early Assessment Program found that nearly 60 percent of the forty thousand newly admitted first-year students required remedial course work in English, mathematics, or both on their arrival. These twenty-five thousand students had taken the college preparatory courses in their high schools and had all received B averages. The program reports that "these students are seemingly confused by having done the right things in high school, only to find out after admission to the CSU that they needed further preparation."[15]

The stories of Henry and Christina capture how students who are enrolled in low-performing schools, and who need the most from school instruction, are getting the least. While many expressed an interest in technology, knowing that it was changing their world, they had little to no exposure to the field, the courses they should be taking to gain expertise, or what they should (or even could) be learning beyond elementary computing skills. "Cutting and pasting" and typing were often identified with the computing curriculum, and there was little understanding of computational thinking and how it differs from these rudimentary skills. There was little or no guidance for students such as Henry and Christina around technology or postsecondary education at East River, and as a result, neither was aware of the preparation required for their educational or career goals. Henry, for example, told us that he has had no formal college counseling and thinking about college made him "dizzy." Indeed, our interview with Henry was held in the college counseling office, and he told us it was the first time he had ever visited the space.

Without opportunities to be introduced to college-preparatory-level work in computer science, it is hard to imagine that Henry's and Christina's plans to pursue it as a career will not be dashed, especially when their college peers may have had much more rigorous instruction in their more-resourced high schools. A study of Chicano scholars who came from low-income families with parents with low levels of education makes clear the importance of these schooling opportunities. Researcher Patricia Gándara (1995) examined a diverse set of factors—including parental support, personal characteristics (such as persistence and ability), and learning opportunities—that contributed to her subjects' success. She found that the most decisive and critical factor was being provided the opportunity to succeed, and that without it, "parental support, persistence, and some adequate level of ability still would not have been sufficient" (113). The two kinds of opportunity that Gándara showed were key were participating in a college preparatory curriculum, and having access to the information and resources that make a college education a realizable goal (113). Yet in a finding that made us extremely disheartened about the rudimentary computing curriculum at East River and all that it indicates, including the accounts of East River students who were being dumped into service or floristry, Gándara discovered that in spite of her subjects' tremendous potential, and in spite of the fact that they were "good students" to begin with, almost *one-third* of the scholars she interviewed were initially destined for vocational courses, which would have effectively foreclosed the opportunity to go to college. [16] Had they not had the opportunity to change their paths, they would not have achieved the success that they did. It is not difficult to see, then, what this means for students like Christina and Henry.

### Opportunities Produce Interest

As we described earlier, East River is a school filled with contradictions and obstacles. It has a dedicated staff of educators, some of whom, as we will see in a moment, are passionately committed to higher-end learning for their students, and others who believe, as we have already discussed, that the lower-level curriculum matches the students' motivations and capacities. It is a school filled with technology and yet it is empty in terms of opportunities to learn computer science. Its overcrowded structure means that students must suffer a more chaotic learning environment that limits their options. Despite all of the barriers, two endeavors at East River illustrate how students remain motivated, and how interest can be generated by dedicated teachers and through quality learning opportunities. Two pairs of educators—one in the mathematics department, and one in the literature department—serve as examples.

### Calculus during Intersession

Two mathematics teachers at East River have developed a program where they each follow a cohort of honors mathematics students over four years with the ultimate goal of preparing them for AP calculus. These teachers acknowledge the large size of East River, and in an attempt to minimize the disruption of the multitrack system and loss of instructional time, they work with the students during the intersessions that occur when the students (and sometimes the teachers) are officially "off-track." Without classroom space during this off-track time, the mathematics classes often meet in the cafeteria or outside in the quad. Contrary to the biased lore about "unmotivated" Latino/as, almost all the invited students choose to come to these intersessions and find them helpful. As Julia, one of the students, notes, "When I started East River, I was getting a C in math, but then I started coming to intersessions and I really got into it. I understood everything they said. They really just got me to like it." As a result of this program, the students and teachers we talked with had positive relationships that transcended the frantic nature of the school calendar. Many of the students we interviewed from these classes spoke to the influence of this "ethic of care."[17] Over half of the young students in the group expressed a desire to pursue careers as mathematics educators, either at the high school level or, for one student, Natalie, at the college level. Natalie's enthusiasm kept her undaunted by what she had decided would be a long-term commitment to get a PhD—an achievement that based on her own research, would "probably take me twelve years or more."

Indeed, what is happening in the East River mathematics program could be happening schoolwide, and it could be happening in the computer science courses. While it is often argued (whether explicitly or implicitly) that schools *would* offer appropriate opportunities (such as a full range of computer science classes or other rigorous course work), *if* and *when* their students are interested and capable, our findings provide the key evidence of reverse causation. We have witnessed how the availability of quality opportunities *produces* interested and capable students. The corollary is also true: the lack of opportunities leaves students with little interest, understanding, and preparation. And hence, a broad cycle of inequality is perpetuated.

**Video Production: Engagement with No Next Step**

Another hopeful instructional story at East River occurs in the video production class. In one of the few noncomputer classes that make use of technology, the two teachers offer students a space to create short videos. These students are placed in working groups to create storyboards and scripts for, act in, produce, and eventually generate films using complex computer applications. This class is immensely popular, and students talked about being "hooked into computing" through the use of video-editing software. We believe that this video production class is a wonderful example of the ways in which technology can be used in a creative context, providing a compelling hook for students.

Unfortunately (and not surprisingly), the organizational constraints of East River limited the effects of this class to a certain degree. At the time of our research, the course instructors were located in the English department and in fact had little interaction with the computer teachers. The technology was not up to par for importing and exporting large files, and resources were limited. Further, teachers in these classes often do not have the necessary computer science knowledge to make a bridge between these application courses and the broader field of computer science. Therefore, as the curriculum stood, the video production content remained somewhat isolated, and there was an absence of classes that could serve as the "next level" for students who wanted to learn more about computing. So while courses like this offer a glimpse into the creative, interdisciplinary possibilities of computing as well as the creativity and interests of students at East River, they also show how there are no opportunities to learn beyond applications-based courses and begin to learn the scientific foundations of the broader field.

## Computer Science Education in High-Poverty Schools

At East River, as at every other school we observed, there were packets of technology-savvy students who had been introduced to computing outside of school. Dora, for instance, is a senior East River student who had a wealth of knowledge about computing, but no opportunity to build on this knowledge at school. Despite the fact that two years earlier she had dropped out of school temporarily, she returned and became a successful mathematics student who learned about programming from an aunt at home. Though Dora is interested in learning more about computer science, she expressed frustration that East River offers no advanced computing classes to further her knowledge: "Well, there's a lot of people [in this school] that are into computers, but they don't take the classes because they feel that it's, like, beneath them. Well, it's pretty much true because half of the classes here are like basic typing and stuff, [and] more than half of everyone knows how to do that anyway."

It is true that students at East River have the opportunity to use computers, and at first glance, this school may seem on par with any "wired" school. But a deeper look reveals that the students are not being introduced even to the fundamental concepts (the *science*) of computer science. At East River, we witnessed computer *skills* being taught in isolation from an understanding of the deeper concepts that underlie them; we saw no connections to other academic subjects, and only the most technologically knowledgeable students were able to demonstrate any understanding of the nature of computer science or its influence on the world. For students interested in pursuing computer science, there was no way to truly engage and no clear path to follow.

As we talked to educators and other interested persons about the structural constraints at East River, we were asked many times, How can you possibly suggest that there is any likelihood that schools like this can offer a rigorous and effective computer science program, considering all the constraints? Further, considering all of the demands on these low-performing schools, Why should it be a priority for them to have computer science in their curriculum? We also asked ourselves these same questions. We now answer these questions in this way: We have seen the interest in technology among East River students. We have talked with students like Christina, Henry, and Dora. Observing the AP calculus program, we have seen the determination, the interest, and what the students are capable of when given a rigorous curriculum and quality preparation—both of which are of tremendous benefit to students because they provide intellectual challenge and, in the case of AP classes, college credit. [18] If these higher-level courses are being offered in schools with high numbers of white and wealthy students (and they are), why is it not a priority to make them available in all schools? Or to use our swimming analogy, if white students are given opportunities to learn to swim in the deepest waters at an early age, how can it possibly be justified that equivalent opportunities are not available for students of color?

Clearly, the road to educational equity does not lie in just adding a programming or AP computer science class to the master schedule at East River. The addition of a single class or teacher will not solve this problem. For quality high school education to occur (in all subjects, not just computer science) students must have powerful learning experiences in a *sequence of classes*, and years of thoughtful, informed guidance and support. Unfortunately, research shows that students in schools such as East River have consistently less access to and are participating less in this high-level and rigorous curriculum across the board. For instance, the College Opportunity Ratio at East River is 100:39:13. This means that for one hundred East River ninth graders, four years later thirty-nine graduated, and only thirteen passed courses required for admission to the

California State University and University of California systems.[19] Further, in 2004 only 9 percent enrolled in community colleges, 5 percent enrolled at California State University campuses, and 2 percent enrolled at the University of California (University of California Accord 2006).

As we write, we continue to be haunted by our conversations and observations at East River. We ponder all the contradictions: the huge unwieldy and overpopulated school; the deficit-thinking beliefs that combine with the school structure to lower the quality of instruction and guidance that students receive; the dedicated teachers, some of whom have committed their lives to the school and the students; and the hardworking, creative, motivated, and intelligent students who are not afforded the education they deserve to achieve their dreams.

We now turn our attention to Westward High School, which is at once similar to East River and yet also quite different. In our exploration of this setting, we see how the underrepresentation in computer science, the obstacles and outcomes that we have begun to explore, become part of the expected—taken for granted, and largely uncontested within the schools.

# 3

# Normalizing the Racial Divide in High School Computer Science

We were drawn to Westward Senior High School because of its purported focus on aerospace, mathematics, and science.[1] We had hoped that as a predominantly African American school with an explicit aerospace program, Westward would provide us a clear window into the experiences of students of color with a technology-rich curriculum. As it turns out (and as often happens in research studies), the story that emerged is far different from what we anticipated at the outset. The story we tell about Westward is instead one of limited expectations and diminished opportunity, and the process by which these limitations escape question.

At Westward, as at East River, we witness how simple technical or digital solutions do not go far enough to address the deep inequities and problems plaguing U.S. schools, because basic equipment must be accompanied by meaningful learning opportunities. Further, we observe how different competencies and interests are linked with different racial groups—for students and educators at Westward High School, computer science has become identified with white and Asian male students. These associations are so ingrained that students, teachers, and administrators alike leave the imbalances unquestioned, as part of the "natural sorting" of interests that occurs among students (Kao 2000). The result is that most students at Westward are denied key resources that would allow them to nurture a curiosity or aptitude for computer science, and this untapped curiosity is then seen as indicative of a lack of innate interest or ability. Ultimately, schools should be the first line of defense against this type of preselected sorting, but instead, as we will see, disparities in educational opportunities further the message that computer science is a field that belongs only to an exclusive set of students.

## Westward Senior High School

Westward Senior High School is located in a predominantly white community, yet because many students come from other neighborhoods, its student population is more diverse. At the time of our research, of Westward's approximately 2,100 students, 64 percent were African American, 26 percent were Latino/a, 7 percent were white, and 2 percent were Asian.[2] The students who attend this school come from a range of socioeconomic backgrounds, although most are working or middle class. Among them are white students who live in the working- and lower-middle-class neighborhood surrounding the school, African American and Latino/a students who travel to the school from lower-income neighborhoods, and African American students who reside in nearby middle-class African American communities—in fact, Westward is one of the Los Angeles public high schools with the highest number of African American middle-class students. So while it is similar to East River in its low percentage of white students, it is somewhat different in terms of socioeconomic indicators. For example, 31 percent of the Westward students participate in the free and reduced-price lunch program (compared to 93 percent of the East River students); 46 percent of the Westward students have one parent who is a college graduate, versus 9 percent at East River.[3]

Over the years, Westward's demographics have changed considerably, as the school has experienced "white flight." A member of our research team, Kimberly Nao, who is African American, had the unusual experience of researching her alma mater. Entering Westward Senior High for the first time since she herself was a student there twenty years ago, Kim felt both a time warp and shock at the change of demographics. The physical structure of the school remained essentially unchanged, with its outdated fixtures and familiar architecture, but one significant transformation had taken place: what was once a predominantly white suburban high school now had a predominantly African American student body. The drop in neighborhood enrollment and the increase in the numbers of students attending the school from other neighborhoods meant that now, twenty years later, Westward is a mainly African American school.

This change in Westward's demographic composition has not gone unnoticed by the parents and teachers who are connected to the school, and in fact, it is an important aspect of the school's culture. One Westward teacher told us that most white families in the neighborhood "look down" on Westward and do not send their children there anymore because "so many kids are bused in." Another noted that because of the population of students who do not live in the immediate community, teachers commonly refer to Westward as a "commuter school." These commuters typically come from neighboring African American communities, and their parents send them to Westward because of its reputation as a rigorous magnet school and because it is safe. This would not be the only contradiction we encountered at Westward, and the contrast between perceptions of quality is at once ironic and heartbreaking.

The fact that Westward is an aerospace math/science magnet suggested to us an interesting context for studying student engagement with technology and computer science curricula. Given the magnet school program, we were hopeful about the curriculum as a whole. Aside from a chapter of Math, Engineering, Science, Achievement (MESA, an outreach program designed to support underrepresented students working toward careers in mathematics and science), the only evidence we saw as we walked around campus of this purported focus on aerospace, however, was one banner from an aerospace corporation hanging in the computer lab (and indeed no aerospace courses were being taught at the school). Artifacts of the athletics culture, on the other hand, were everywhere: banners hanging on display in the hallways, apparel for sale on tables near the front office, and signs throughout campus. At the time, Westward had a championship basketball team; by 2005 it had claimed the state championship three years in a row. Besides the strong presence of sports culture, events on campus—from formal school pep rallies to informal rap sessions at lunchtime—were marked by hip-hop culture, as they are at many urban schools. On one of our visits, lunchtime came alive with an impromptu jam session where students surrounded a group of boys who were engaged in freestyling while others maintained a hip-hop beat by banging a fist or pencil against a bungalow wall.[4]

The energy that Westward derives from sports was in sharp contrast to other aspects of the school's culture. Most unfortunately, if there was one theme that kept reoccurring in our interviews with Westward educators it would be the theme of lack—the lack of qualified (certified) teachers, useful professional development for teachers, stable leadership, resources, and community, and a perceived lack of motivated students. Westward typifies what happens in too many urban schools with high numbers of students of color: low expectations for students, budget constraints, a curriculum buffeted by the winds of external mandates, and a changing vision and direction intensified by the revolving door of principals (at

Westward there had been five in the previous six years). For the last several years, Westward has been classified as a low-performing school.[5]

## No Opportunity to Learn Computer Science

As we began our research, Westward was in the midst of its Digital High School program, receiving state funds for computers intended to bridge the digital divide. Nevertheless, here was one of the many places we again heard the theme of lack. Computers were being distributed to classrooms slowly, one department at a time. Teachers who did have computers in their rooms often had a hard time figuring out what to do with them, and as a result, many students and teachers complained that equipment sat in the back of the room "collecting dust." Frequently, in fact, the machines did not even work. There were no teachers to teach computer classes beyond the introductory level, and there was no sense that it was important anyway. So the problem at Westward was not necessarily the dearth of computers on campus but rather the challenge of supporting and maximizing the use of the computers the school did have. Westward, just like East River, was an example of how hopes hang on technology to be the magic bullet to improve academic achievement. Yet both schools illustrate how access and academic achievement (or the lack of it) are the result of deep structural issues that require much more than a technological solution.

At the start of our project, the only two computer courses offered at Westward were introduction to computers and Internet publishing. The basic introduction to computers course covered PowerPoint and word processing. The Internet publishing class focused on Web design (one section was in charge of constructing the school's Web site), but it was held in a magnet lab with no Internet access. There was no official computer science teacher at Westward so these classes were being taught by a young, uncertified history teacher, Mr. Reyes, who had volunteered to teach the students drawing on his prior experience working as a Web designer. Reyes was a brand-new teacher, well liked by the students, and readily admitted that he was learning how to teach as he went along. He was committed to introducing a diverse group of students to computer skills and wanted to engage them with computing, but was not provided with the tools he needed, such as Internet access, adequate software, professional development opportunities, or a community of teachers to learn from.

A couple of years before our research began, there was one teacher with a computer science background at Westward, but he transferred to a different school. When he was at Westward, the school offered several computer courses including the introductory courses, a networking class, Web design, computer programming, and AP computer science. Yet after this teacher's departure, over a short amount of time, this pipeline of courses was eliminated. When we selected Westward High as a research site in 2000, one course, AP computer science, was still being offered. But by the following year when we began our data collection, it had been canceled. As we had done at East River, we asked, Why was the computer science curriculum eliminated, especially at a time when there is so much concern about the shortage of interest and expertise in math, science, computing, and engineering in this country? As at East River, finances played a large role, but our conversations about the issue also revealed several other facets of the problem.

When we interviewed the Westward principal about the curriculum cutbacks and specifically why the AP computer science class was canceled, she told us how it was initially taken over by a mathematics teacher who had taught AP computer science at a previous high school, but according to the principal, the teacher had trouble "managing the class." The class enrollment eventually dropped to only five students, and none of them passed the AP exam. The students we interviewed who took the course felt that the teacher did not know enough about computer programming to help prepare them for the test. The teacher, on the other hand, felt that due to her race (African American) and gender, the racially diverse yet mostly male students underestimated her ability to teach the subject.[6] Since the students did not have what the principal considered to be "the right teacher" at the time, rather than find someone new, the principal chose to cancel the course altogether. This sits in contrast to what happened when the school's band faced elimination because of the lack of both interest and a qualified teacher. Because of the way band is classified in the school, when students enroll in it, it relieves pressure on other overcrowded courses. So in addition to the principal's feelings that "the band was very important," it was also more central to the organizational goals of Westward. Even though the principal considers AP computer science to be the "apex" of the computing curriculum, when we asked her if she thinks there is a Westward population of students for AP computer science, she replied, "Not yet. I don't think so." So not only did the class have less institutional import than other subjects, it was also not perceived as relevant to the students.

The principal as well as many of the other educators we talked with at Westward made direct or indirect references to the ways in which they perceived their students as "lacking" or unmotivated. We heard explicit references to Westward kids as "spoiled" and "lazy."[7] The principal attributed the trash in the hallways and a recent increase in graffiti to students who are "commuters" (and in her eyes, therefore not connected to the school), and to some who "just come here to rest their heads." Teachers mostly used more circumspect language. For instance, a teacher who was on the Digital High School advisory board referred to the high numbers of Westward students with "lower skills" and those who "are coming from outside, not from local schools," implying they are not as well prepared as they should be. She then described a dilemma that concerns many educators in diverse schools:

You're trying to work with those kids who are coming in [with] lower skills, to bring them up to par, and to work with those who are at [a] skill level that is commensurate with where they're supposed to be, and bringing them up higher and enriching them. . . . it's a two-pronged thing. Where do we put our resources, you know?

Where to put Westward's personnel and budget resources was the problem that the principal also referred to as she described eliminating the computer science curriculum at the school: "We don't have the personnel and we can't afford the personnel."

In light of AP computer science being canceled, we talked with the Westward principal about her current vision for the computer science program for Westward students. In a comment that echoes the priorities of the East River principal, she told us that in the end, when the Westward students graduate, she just wants them to be "functional":

I just want kids to be able, when they leave here, to be functional, because part of analyzing a situation is getting the data that you need. The data is now on the Internet. You can go to libraries all you want, but sometimes it's just easier to access the data from the Internet and to understand, Is it a valid source? Is it a current source? Is somebody trying to sell me something? So I think that they need to have that awareness also.

Indeed, learning media literacy and being functional in information management skills is critical for all students today. But it should be the floor. At a time when the cognitive bar for new jobs is being raised, when problem-solving knowledge and computational thinking are transforming all disciplines, students should have learning opportunities that introduce them to thinking and science beyond a functional level. Based on our observations at Westward as well as at East River, it seems that in schools with high numbers of students of color, where courses in technology do exist, higher-order skills have been stripped out of the curriculum. In keeping with the historical tendencies of vocational education, only elementary "follow directions" and "cut-and-paste" instruction remain, and learning opportunities that could take students beyond these basics were nowhere to be found. In this way, the stories of East River and Westward were disturbingly similar. For any student at either of these schools who wanted to learn more about computer science, there simply were no opportunities to learn about the higher-order problem solving that typifies it. This lack of access was blamed largely on structural constraints (the absence of the right teacher, budget shortages, or testing priorities), and the pervasive indifference to it was justified by a perceived lack of interest or ability on the part of the students.

**Interest But No Place to Hang and Learn**

In spite of the widespread belief among teachers and administrators that computer science was not a priority for students, and that the curiosity and capacity simply were not there, we continued to observe students who were interested in technology and wanted to do more with it. During our time in the Internet publishing classroom, despite the fact that the course was reputed to be a dumping ground for students who needed an elective, there were clusters of students, mostly males, who had developed an outside interest in computing through relatives or friends, and wanted to learn more. The comments from these students speak volumes about the potential interest in computer science at Westward.

Pablo, a Latino student, had come to Westchester for the aerospace magnet and was disappointed that there were actually no classes having to do with aerospace at the school. With a father who is a teacher and former pilot, Pablo described himself as a "self-taught computer whiz" and was interested in computing as it relates to airplane design. Greg, an African American student, told us about his uncle, who works with hardware and programming, and helped Greg get the parts to try building his own computer. Brian, who is also African American, spoke of designing medical equipment. Another African American student, Brad, talked about using computers to compose music. In a mathematics analysis class we interviewed Brandon, yet another African American student, who described his passions as playing guitar, weight lifting, and learning calculus, particularly "not just the calculus itself, but how calculus can be used in engineering." Brandon told us that engineering was going to be his college major, because "I think it's interesting how buildings like this can last forever or fifty years without crashing down because engineering was used." While most of the self-identified "techie" students were males, there were some females as well. For instance, Maxine told us that she would be attending the University of California at Riverside and wanted to get involved with computers once she is there. She is the "technology person" in the school leadership class, loves "putting things together," and has spent time reconstructing old computers that her dad brings home from work.

These are just a few of the students who stand in contradiction to the principal's assumption that her students would not have sufficient interest to warrant a full computer science curriculum. In fact, approximately 30 percent of the students we interviewed self-identified as being techies. Yet just as at East River, for a Westward student who had an interest in engaging in more rigorous classroom learning of computer science or being exposed to problem solving in the field, the opportunities were not there. And not only did formal course work not exist but informal learning opportunities were scarce too.

Of the three computer labs on campus, two were limited to class time only, and one had been open intermittently at lunch. A group of students, predominantly African American males, used this lab at lunchtime to work on various projects, such as designing home Web pages, playing games, and creating sites for selling things. Yet ultimately even this limited access was curtailed. According to the teacher in charge of technology, student "mischief" on the computers, or at least activity that was perceived as such (game playing, altering the desktop, and viewing inappropriate material on the one computer that did have Internet access), caused the administration to close the computer labs down during lunch. As a result, with a shortage of classes, a shortage of adults who were knowledgeable about computer science, and no place at the school for students to learn from one another and network with peers interested in technology, computer science culture and learning were stymied.[8]

There was one important exception to this at Westward: the Computer Science Service Bureau, an official group of the most tech-savvy students in the school that was pulled together by the Digital High School coordinator to help her troubleshoot equipment problems, begin the process of building a Web site, and install software. In this predominantly African American school, most of these Service Bureau students were white (and all but one were male), and all had learned their skills at home and were eager to practice on the school equipment. These students were proud of their jobs and identity as the school tech squad, seeing themselves as having a crucial role in the school. One of the most active of the group, Derek, talked to us about the need to protect the school equipment. He told us, "We have to kind of protect ourselves because people try to come in and cause harm, and then we have to work and fix it, so we just solve this by blocking them out and using their own stupidity against them." When the interviewer said "OK, OK, so you guys hang out there to kind of guard the lab?" Derek replied, "Yeah, we're kind of sentries." Without necessarily intending to, Derek had revealed the sharp division that Westward students and teachers perceive between those who "do technology" and those who do not.

### Being Really, Really Smart to Be in Computer Science

The perception that one must be smart, "really, really smart," to do computer science is widely held among students and teachers, and as we will discuss in a moment, perceptions of who is smart enough often fall along racial lines. When asked what her image of a computer scientist is, for example, Mariele, a Latina student, described them as "an intelligent person, very disciplined." Similarly, talking about the kids in the school who know the most about computers, Renee, who is African American, said, "I would hope that everybody in this school is an intellectual, but [computer science types] seem more intellectual."

Adults in the school also shared these expectations of who does computer science and what type of students will do well in the field. Mr. Henry, for instance, is a white AP calculus teacher at Westward. While he himself does not know programming or computer science, his model of a computer scientist comes from people he observed in graduate school and more recently from observations of his own son. Describing his own graduate school acquaintances who were computer science majors, he painted a portrait of individuals consumed with the subject matter:

Some of the people, they would always seem to be in the computer room 'til six or seven in the morning, it'd be open twenty-four hours a day. [They] would be the ones that were in there all night long and [they've] got to love it. Their social life might be there, but it'd be sort of sporadic and kind of their own thing, you know, and not like meeting at six for dinner. That may not happen 'cause they may not eat 'til breakfast.

Henry now sees similar behavior in his teenage son, who is involved with computing. Watching his son and his son's friends, Henry has developed a schema for what type of student he believes will do well in computer science. Of primary importance, in Henry's view, is that "you need to be pretty bright to go into that field and it seems like you have to have a love of it, I suppose, to want to do it, and I don't know that that many people do." When we asked Henry how his son got into computing, he said that his son "learned it on his own," and Henry believes that this self-starter quality is also something that defines computer science students: "And from what I've seen, a lot of the kids that do have that interest, they take the books [about computers] . . . and that's how they learn how to study." He associates all of these qualities with the "really bright kids," noting that someone in computer science has to have a lot of patience to stick with a problem and figure it all out. He describes his son, who will sit in front of the computer ten to twelve hours a day, and how Henry has to work hard to get him away from the computer to go take a run and be active. But from it all, Henry maintains that "not everybody can do that, so I think it takes a special person."

Comments from Westward students also provide great insight into what type of person is perceived as "special" enough to pursue computer science. For many students, intelligence, when linked with a particular racial group, was most commonly linked with whites and Asians, and many drew on unfortunate (but common) stereotypes to communicate their thoughts. Fernando, who is Latino, described a typical computer scientist this way: "A dude with some real glasses, talking weird. . . . [T]hey'll probably be white or Chinese, 'cause they're, like, smart and they like those things." A Latino student commented about the Asians in his AP calculus course, saying, "I wish I could have their brains, as in AP calculus class, they have everything done and, like, they are just sitting there waiting for the next thing to happen." Students specifically mentioned whites and Asians going to Saturday classes, and how "they are into learning more about different things than [are] African Americans or Hispanics." One African American student talked about East Indians in the technology industry and about education being important in the Indian culture, comparing East Indian students to Asians, who "go to school six days a week; they are good at math." Then, reflecting on his thoughts, he added, "Now, that's a stereotype."

Sadly, these stereotypes also exist among the educators at Westward, many of whom do not view the majority of their students as "special" or "really bright kids." Overall, as we reported earlier, we more often encountered spoken and unspoken inferences about Westward students being unmotivated or else lacking in the capacity to handle a course such as AP computer science. These are, unfortunately, the expectations and evaluations widely heard in low-performing schools (Oakes and Guiton 1995), and as we discussed in the previous chapter, they are compounded by a long history in this country of a racialized hierarchy of academic and intellectual potential, in which African American and Latino/a students are regularly thought of as at the bottom (Gould 1996; Oakes and Lipton 2007, 172; Oakes, Wells, Datnow, and Jones 1997; Perry, Steele, and Hilliard 2003; Pollock 2004; Solórzano and Ornelas 2002). Westward students are keenly aware of not only this hierarchy but also the range of additional factors—from economics to a lack of role models—that have contributed to its construction.

## Economics and Access

As we spoke with students at Westward about why they thought there were proportionately fewer Latino/a and African American students in the computer science pipeline, they frequently mentioned the contribution of inequalities in both finances and equipment. Lindsay, who is African American, pointed to the fact that "Caucasians usually have more affluence and better access to computers" as a reason for lower levels of interest among her peers. This increased access, as Lindsay astutely noted, means that "they have been able to discover that they have an interest in them and how they can have fun with them, and not just use them for more technical things." Stephen, who is also African American, echoed this point, making an important further distinction: "It's not just race but the demographics of people who live in poverty, or in the inner city, are usually black, Hispanic." His comments are very much in keeping with the themes of this book, as he at once touches on the issues of race, SES, access, and interest:

I mean, not that they are not interested in computers, but computers are very expensive and they may not be able to afford a computer or fast enough computer to allow them to enjoy computers as much as, you know, somebody who lives in the suburbs. . . . So, it would be a white man, I would say. . . . The same family, if you took them out of Inglewood and placed them into some place like Bel Air, then they'd probably have the same interests.

Another student, Carlos, who is Latino, was also acutely aware that access determines interest, and that in general, the "white people and the Asian people, they are in the communities with more money, more chances." Although Carlos acknowledged that some African Americans and Latino/as do also enjoy these same resources, he recognized that by and large, "they don't have as many opportunities because they don't have as much money like the others." Ultimately, Carlos pinpointed the unfairness of the system, and in doing so, addressed one of the core reasons we explored this topic in the first place: "You could have a really smart person who doesn't have any money, or who has the potential to be really smart and all that, but because of lack of money they can't get up to the same level as somebody else with the same IQ or whatever, just living in a richer neighborhood."

What was particularly striking and disheartening about these remarks from Westward students was the fact that in spite of their clear insights into the ways in which their own aspirations as well as computing experiences were being limited, they did not seem particularly bothered by it. Instead, their comments revealed the ways in which demographic inequities in computer science are all but expected.

### Role Models

In addition to economic disparities and access differences, students also discussed how they rarely see people who look like them involved in computing, and this lack of role models is a significant factor in decisions about whether or not to pursue technology. Nia, an African American student who is quoted in our introduction, explained how the images that do exist make it look like the field is "geared toward whites." While she does feel that people can "step up to the plate" and "anyone can do anything," she is not immune to the images of computer science that make it "look like only Caucasians should be in that industry":

I think minorities are limited, not only because of their background and where they come from, but also most ethnicities are stuck in where they were in the past. They are scared to jump into the future because what it looks like is only

Caucasians should be in that industry. But it's not really true. Anyone can do anything. But I don't know. I guess it's the same thing as stepping up to the plate. And maybe they don't think that they belong or they just limit themselves.

These media-savvy students are critical consumers of a wide range of marketing messages, including television advertisements, which by and large also lack a diversity of role models. Stephen, an African American student, described how even on "black television, the television shows that black people watch the most," the advertisements that have to do with technology are "geared more toward white people," with white actors, and according to Stephen, exhibit little relevance to his everyday life.

For many, computer science role models are "computer nerds" who do more to create barriers to interest than foster its development. For instance, Lisa, an African American student, talked about the "stereotypes we've created among ourselves" and the fear that she perceives among African Americans of being seen as a geek. The result, in her eyes, is that her peers are not likely to "be particularly open to" learning how to work with computers. Another student, Allison, who is white and was the only female member of the Computer Science Service Bureau, shared Lisa's perceptions, and had definite theories about different racial groups' relationships to technology in the school:

It's generally more acceptable to see a white nerd than a black nerd, and, I mean, it's cultural to some degree. I'm rather unbiased about it, but from just what I see, there are generally a lot more Caucasians in technology fields and who spend quite a lot of their time on it, especially like in this school, as you see, there are only a few African Americans that really know their stuff and they're pretty dang good at that. I wouldn't really call it racism or anything, or like not being accepted, just not many of them seem to be interested in it. And the ones that are, we welcome with open arms.

What Allison concludes about African Americans and computer science bears repeating: "just not many of them seem to be interested in it" and this is "cultural to some degree." Allison's remarks capture a prevalent viewpoint that pervades the halls of Westward about the racial gap in computer science: it comes down to interest, ability, and culture—some have it, and some do not.

Although many students shared Lisa's and Allison's views, it is worth noting that some did contest them. Rhonda, an African American student, told us that even though she does not see being a computer nerd as part of the "being big and bad" category, she knows African American students who would pursue the field anyway:

I don't see us knowing how to do the things like programming or learning stuff like that. Why? For some reason a lot of blacks I know have got this idea that they have to be big and they have to be bad and whatever, and I don't see being a computer nerd [as] part of that little category. . . . I know people who would do that; they really couldn't care less what anyone else is thinking.

And Greg, who is also African American and very much interested in computer science, observed:

It's because our society may think it's not hip . . . it's not rap, it's not hip-hop. I think that's the main reason because they're just scared of what people might say if somebody found out they're really into computers. Me, I don't care if they know I like computers. I tell people I built my own computer. But some people, I tell 'em I have a Web site. Everybody says, "Oh, it's cool." They tell me they want to get into stuff like that, but they never really do it because of their fear or whatever.

So while Rhonda and Greg provide a counter to the stereotype, it is nevertheless crucial to point out that even when students are willing to break from what they perceive as the norm (or when they believe others would), they are also aware of the fact that they are doing it with limited role models and social support, making a challenging endeavor even more difficult.[9]

### Westward as a Sports School

As we described earlier, Westward has a strong athletic program, with a particular emphasis on basketball. One female student we spoke with summed it up well:

The thing about Westward High School is it's really, really sports oriented. The administration might not want that to be the case. They give out academic jackets instead of lettermen's jackets, but they are definitely really sports oriented. Most [other] people, they hang out on the senior lawn or down at the cafeteria and talk about music, movies, guys, girls. I mean [here] it's just sports, sports, sports, oh my gosh, sports.

Because of Westward's strong athletic program, along with its high concentration of African American students, our visits to this campus made us think more about different domains and how they are linked to different individuals. Computer techies and basketball hoopsters both have expert identities, and both activities have become highly identified with different racial groups. Princeton University professor of philosophy K. Anthony Appiah (2000), in his essay "Racial Identity and Racial Identification," discusses how basketball, like jazz or hip-hop, "belongs to an African American, whether she likes it or knows anything about it, because it is culturally marked as Black" (cited in Ogden and Hilt 2003, 612).

While we were not in a position to conduct a full study of identity and sports, we believed that there was much to learn from this topic and therefore read as much as we were able to on it. One article, "The Collective Identity and Basketball: An Explanation of the Decreasing Number of African Americans on America's Baseball Diamonds" (Ogden and Hilt 2003), sparked our thinking about how basketball emerged as the preeminent African American sport, how it has become "culturally marked" as African American, and how the presence (and absence) of different "facilitators" paved the way for these developments. These facilitators include access to facilities and resources, role models in the field, encouragement from adults, and the promise of social mobility. [10] Their existence over time has led to basketball becoming a sport and cultural space where many young African Americans develop expertise, feel fully accepted, and are empowered. [11]

After thinking about these issues, we were particularly struck by two things. First, despite the ongoing contributions of these economic and social facilitators to racial patterns in basketball, assumptions about the innate characteristics of African Americans in the sport have become part of the deep-seated beliefs in our country.[12] Second, the key facilitators for basketball are the same ones that one would expect (or hope) to see in education, yet few (if any) are in place for students of color interested in studying computer science. Viewing schools like Westward and East River through this lens, we would hope to see access to a full sequence of computer science courses, informal learning communities with role models and student support, and a culture that has high expectations for the academic capacities of students of color. And yet we saw little, if any, evidence that these facilitators existed. And so we wondered, What does this do to the ways in which students view their own potential and self-efficacy in this domain?

## Group Categorization in Schools

Research from Chicago public schools has been useful for helping us understand what we were seeing at Westward. In a study titled "Group Images and Possible Selves among Adolescents: Linking Stereotypes to Expectations by Race and Ethnicity" (Kao 2000), a group of researchers conducted interviews and focus groups with high school students to document how social categories are linked to behavior norms in high schools. They found that schools are filled with deeply held and often unconscious beliefs about "essential" (such as biological, cultural, and familial) differences between different ethnic groups. And so although schools are supposed to be the "great equalizers," they are instead institutions where different groups are continually compared and ranked.

While social categories such as "jocks," "burnouts," "nerds," and "popular kids" have long been linked to behavioral norms in high schools (Coleman 1961; Eckert 1989), this Chicago school study found that students of color face an additional dimension of social categorization: students of all ethnic and racial backgrounds link group images of ethnicity to different innate abilities, and these images "not only directly imply norms of behavior for members of each group, but also specify their distinct areas of expertise in various realms of social and academic life" (Kao 2000, 408). Specifically, the study found that Asians are thought of as being good in mathematics and science, destined to rule the business world, and associated with computers; whites are seen as good students, doing their homework, "nerdy," and well educated; African Americans are perceived of as being good in sports, not doing well in school, and less likely to be in honors classes; and Latino/as are thought of as not doing well in school because of a lack of effort, while being on the track for manual labor.[13]

Although students and teachers articulate many of the stereotypes just outlined, schools are also commonly filled with *unspoken* assumptions. This means that even when race is not mentioned specifically, descriptors of different competencies and interests are enough to trigger the "race label." For instance, when phrases like "really smart" or "good in math and science" are used, it is Asians and whites who are imagined; with "lacking motivation," "lazy," or even "urban," it is African Americans and Latino/as who come to mind.[14] Just the mention of a school's demographics triggers race connotations and judgments among educators about ability; the mostly African American Westward campus does not escape these tendencies.

In addition to the differences in how groups are evaluated in terms of academic ability and tendencies, the Chicago study also found that in heterogeneous schools, different ethnic groups dominated different extracurricular activities. Many of the students interviewed told researchers about occasions when they either did not join or withdrew from a particular club or sport because of the "strong association of certain ethnic groups with particular activities" (Kao 2000, 424). Most important for our work, the study found how students perceived these activities as a "natural sorting mechanism": "since anyone can join any activity, and since activity X is composed primarily of Whites, then Whites must be especially able at activity X" (426). As the researchers conclude, "Images of group competencies and patterns of racial segregation in extracurricular activities work hand-in-hand to legitimatize beliefs that groups differ in their interests and abilities" (425).

This flawed logic goes well beyond the world of extracurricular activities (like basketball) and most certainly plays out in the world of computing, where the assumption is that computers are everywhere so either you are into them or you are not, and your daily interactions with technology must be indicative of the side on which you fall. And so patterns of enrollment and participation in computer science serve to create and sustain the notion that the underrepresentation of students of color is occurring because of different innate interests and abilities. And without a doubt, this notion of natural sorting and what is supposedly normal takes a toll on students and their perceptions of themselves.

## The Underrepresentation in Computer Science as an Indicator of Larger Inequities

Our conversations with students and educators at Westward revealed some of the ways in which structural issues along with the culture of a school (expectations in particular) play major roles in shaping students' views of where they will (or will not) fit. In her book *Can We Talk about Race?* Beverly Tatum raises a series of important questions that are highly relevant to our inquiry into the racial divide in computer science and has helped us to frame our own analysis of these issues. Tatum asks, "How do students see themselves reflected in their school environments? What stories are being told about who they are? What messages are being transmitted to them in their daily interactions in the classrooms and in the school hallways, and by whom?" (2007, 24). Moreover, "if we think about school environments as an illustrated book in which students look to see themselves, we have to ask, what story is being told, and who is included in the illustrations? . . . What does this mean for their own view about their possibilities, their future?" She further asks, "Is there a relationship between invisibility in the curriculum and the underachievement of Black and Latino students?" (29).

Tatum's questions are the larger frame around our own: What does it suggest to students of color when a field such as computer science is highly segregated? What does it indicate when they never see images of people who look like them associated with the field? What does it mean for a school of predominantly African American students that their school has an aerospace magnet program, but no courses in aerospace or computer science? What does it suggest when a school offers fewer rigorous courses than are offered at wealthier schools with higher concentrations of white students? What does this perpetuate in terms of students' sense of their academic identities and the worlds that they should consider?[15] The answers to these questions speak volumes about the ongoing contradictions in our school system—a system that purports to provide an equal playing field, but in actuality is mired in deeply held, often stereotypical beliefs about students' abilities. If certain students are perceived of as intellectual and logical, while others are perceived of as naturally kinesthetic, these stereotypes (no matter how subtly expressed) will likely color both the choices students make for themselves and the choices that others make for them.

At both East River and Westward, we observed how educators' evaluations of the interests and abilities of the predominantly Latino/a and African American students did not match the qualities that educators assumed necessary for interest in computer science to develop, and for students to excel in the subject. Further, white and Asian males apparently just enjoy computer science more than others do, or so the mind-set goes. But this attribution is problematic, for it in essence lets our educational system off the hook by placing responsibility for the underrepresentation on the shoulders of its students. It assumes that interest and ability are not only innate but also fixed.[16] How, we wondered, could schools such as East River and Westward possibly measure interest in computer science when these two schools had nothing even remotely resembling computer science in their curriculum? While a lack of interest might be a convenient excuse to drop a course that proved to be difficult to staff or populate, this rationale is not based in fact. Instead, structural inequalities, including home and school learning opportunities as well as school culture and expectations, are continuously shaping identities and interests, and in turn, participation in the field of computer science.

These issues of access and race are not even remotely limited to the field of computer science. Broader trends of exclusion point out the widespread problems in our schools. The annual statistics of Westward students taking advanced mathematics, for example, show distinct differences between racial groups that mimic the patterns in the computer science field.[17] In 2006–7, 38 percent of the Asian ninth- through twelfth-grade students at Westward enrolled in advanced mathematics classes, as did 30 percent of the white students. In sharp contrast, only 5 percent of the African American students and 4 percent of the Latino/a students did so.[18] This is shocking in any context, but particularly in a school with a predominantly African American and Latino/a population. Further, during the 2005–6 time frame, only 51 percent of the Westward mathematics teachers had the appropriate credentials to teach college preparatory mathematics, which limits the number of courses that can be offered.[19] Finally, the College Opportunity Ratio, an indicator of a school's effectiveness in preparing students for college, gives Westward a score of 100:47:16. This shows that for every one hundred ninth-grade students, four years later only forty-seven have graduated, and only sixteen have passed courses required for admission to the California State University or University of California systems.[20]

Clearly, when studying why so few African American and Latino/a students are pursuing computer science, it is critical to understand the entire school context. We have explored what happens in overcrowded, underfunded schools with high concentrations of students of color. What about schools with better funding and a larger proportion of white students? In our next chapter, we continue to examine the interaction of structural inequities with belief systems at our third school—a relatively well-resourced school with a diverse population of students (including a higher percentage of white students) and a full pipeline of computer science courses. We see how these same structural and individual factors interact in different ways, and yet yield the same outcome: the underrepresentation of students of color in computer science.

# 4

## Claimed Spaces: "Preparatory Privilege" and High School Computer Science

Nestled in the hills overlooking the Pacific Ocean, in a predominantly white and wealthy community, sits Canyon Charter High School. In contrast to the crowded hallways of East River and the concrete surroundings of Westward, this school has a more open, airy feel. The school buildings form a square around a large center quad, a green, open-air space where students gather during nutrition breaks, breathing the ocean air while soaking in the sunshine. This is a school with a lot to offer its students. Canyon was recently recognized as a California Distinguished School, and was named by *Newsweek* magazine as in the top 1 percent of U.S. high schools. Its wealth of resources and opportunities are in part due to the dedicated teachers and administrators who have been at the school for many years, but they are also a reflection of the power and wealth of the Canyon neighborhood parents who are well connected and well resourced, and who use those assets to help increase the caliber of their children's education.

Canyon's strong academic record draws students from all over the city, enrolling students from over a hundred zip codes through its mathematics and science magnet and charter schools. As a result, Canyon has a diverse school population, despite the relatively homogeneous demographics of its neighborhood. At the time of our study (the 2001–2 and 2002–3 school years), approximately 43 percent of the students were white, 24 percent were African American, 24 percent were Latino/a, and 8 percent were Asian American/Pacific Islander. It is also the school in our study with the smallest percentage of students who qualify for free or reduced-price lunches (27 percent) as well as the smallest percentage of students who are not yet English proficient (only 7 percent). Moreover, of the three schools in our study, the parents of Canyon students have the highest number of years of formal education: 81 percent have some college education (versus 55 percent countywide), and 63 percent have a college degree (compared with just 34 percent countywide).[1] This is a school with a reputation for high achievement and a college-going culture.

As at our other school sites, technological resources are plentiful at Canyon: there are several computer labs on campus, and every nontechnology-oriented classroom has at least four computers in it. Technologically speaking, Canyon has an active Digital High School program, but this is where the similarities end. Unlike at East River or Westward, Canyon has a knowledgeable computer science teaching staff and a comparatively large number of students with previous computing experience. Courses range from introductory computers to AP computer science. The AP computer science teacher had owned her own software design business and worked for years as a programmer. And while technology *competency* is different from computer *science*, Canyon is the only school in our study that has its own technology competency requirement for graduation. To fulfill it, students must take and pass one of the following technical courses: information processing, computer programming (in Visual Basic), AP computer science, business education, introduction to media arts, advanced media, graphic arts/desktop, or yearbook. Canyon High School has a New Media Entertainment Academy where students learn to use new media technologies (computers, video, Internet, 3-D animation, etc.). The academy works with community partners in the new media and entertainment industries, affording students internships and job opportunities in the new media field. As a consequence, and in sharp contrast to the military recruiters often seen at East River, when recruiters do come to visit Canyon, they are from Web design companies and Hollywood movie studios that offer summer internship programs as part of their community service programs.

Because of the diverse population and wide range of computer science classes offered at Canyon, the school provided us the unique opportunity to learn more about a diverse group of students' experiences with the subject beyond the introductory level. Because of its diverse student population and school resources, Canyon was also the one school in our study most poised to broaden participation in computing, to shift the paradigm. Yet as we soon discovered, while Canyon offered an assortment of technology courses, there was a marked demographic shift as one moved up the computer science pipeline. While entry-level computing classes, such as data processing, had a diverse student population, in AP computer science there was a notable absence of students of color.

Over the three-year period of our research, only two African American students enrolled in the course, and one dropped out halfway through the first semester; the number of Latino/a students was only slightly higher. And it is worth mentioning that while there is no gender imbalance in the overall enrollment at Canyon, males made up, on average, 84 percent of the AP computer science student classroom.

In this chapter, we examine how the Canyon computer science pipeline becomes less diverse as the courses become more advanced. In doing so, we explain how students' enrollment decisions are embedded in larger school and social dynamics. We came to realize through this research that while interest and choice are ordinarily framed as individual and personal actions, this is not an adequate understanding. Instead, the ways in which students make their decisions are, again, largely determined by structural factors and widely held beliefs, even in a school where opportunities abound. And all of these issues are still very much intertwined with the larger ones of race, class, and gender.

The story we tell about Canyon is markedly different from those of Westward and East River. At Westward and East River, the courses we were most interested in exploring simply weren't there, making it nearly impossible for us in that context to tell the story of students of color in computer science. The story that instead evolved was one focused more on how the complexities of an overcrowded, underresourced institution preclude the existence of a computer science curriculum. Our experience at Canyon sits in sharp contrast, for at Canyon there were higher-level computer science course offerings. Our challenge was to understand why so few students of color enroll in them.

## The Whole School Context: A Segregated "Integrated" School

The strength of Canyon's reputation is evidenced by the sacrifices that out-of-neighborhood students make in order to attend this school. The majority of "traveling" students are students of color who apply to Canyon through its mathematics and science magnet program. They tell us stories of having to wake up at 5:00 a.m. in order to get to their school buses on time. Los Angeles public transit is not an option for many of these students because it can be cumbersome and extremely time-consuming, so they are tied to a particular schedule, and thus, they often cannot fully participate in things like extracurricular activities or even just hanging out with other students. While these are major sacrifices for high school students, they and their families feel it is worth it because Canyon provides them a better education than they would receive in their neighborhood schools.

While most students told us that all of the different groups of students "get along," they also said (and we observed) that during lunch and nutrition breaks, students tend to hang out with people of their same ethnic or racial background, typically in completely separate physical locations. Student conjectures about why this separation exists varied widely. Some thought it occurs because students prefer to socialize with people who attended their own middle schools or live in their same neighborhoods. Others said that being with people from the same ethnic background is an issue of comfort. Several students pointed out that even if they wanted to, it would be difficult for traveling students to be friends with the Canyon "neighborhood kids" because of the distance between their homes. Many students simply said they did not know why students are socially separated.

Disturbingly, while traveling students of color make extreme sacrifices to attend this better-resourced and reputed school, relatively few benefit from its accelerated offerings. Despite the recent accolades for Canyon's academic achievement, the school typifies what has been noted in other educational research as "two schools in one" (Noguera 2003). "Regular" classes are heavily populated by students of color, whereas the advanced and honors courses are predominantly white and Asian. While Canyon has 50 percent students of color, only 10 percent were in the honors classes during the time of our research. Given this divide in both its academic and social arenas, it should come as no surprise that the advance-level computer science courses at Canyon are likewise segregated.

In this chapter we discuss how, in a school setting as diverse as Canyon, advanced computer science remains insular, dominated primarily by white (male) students.[2] We first examine the disengaging curriculum of the "feeder" course, computer programming, and show how it not only fails to actually feed a diverse body of students into the pipeline but also can turn students *off* to computer science altogether. In the next part of the chapter, we turn our focus to Canyon's AP computer science course, and investigate which students enroll, why they enroll, and what the classroom environment is like for the students who are outside the norm. We show how AP computer science becomes the claimed "marked territory" of a narrow substratum of students who come from families and communities with home resources that give them a jump-start into computer science well before they enter Canyon High. And by examining why so few students of color enroll in advanced and honors classes in general, we learn even more about why high school computer science continues to be an insular and segregated course of study, and how individual choices must be understood as the result of influences that extend well beyond the desires of the single student.

### Disengaging Curriculum: Failing to Capitalize on Computer Science Hooks

Computer programming is one of the electives at Canyon that qualifies as a technical art and fulfills that particular graduation requirement; as such, the class is large and diverse. A full 40 percent of the students we interviewed enrolled in the course not because of interest but because it was the only thing that fit into their schedules to meet the technology requirement or because their first (and sometimes second) elective choices were full. Still, a majority of the students who enrolled did so because of some interest in the subject, and yet few who took programming moved on to study AP computer science. So already we begin to see the narrowing of the computer science pipeline. The question is, *Why?*

Unfortunately, the programming class highlights how poorly imagined and defined the computer science curriculum is at the high school level. Even though the programming course at Canyon was significantly more developed than the course at East River, the curriculum was still textbook based, narrowly focused on syntax and following directions, and consisted of students reading a textbook about programming along with assignments that were based on copying programs outlined in the book. The programming assignments, even at the end of the year when the basic concepts had been established, were relatively simple, for instance, asking students to create programs in Visual Basic that would calculate their age in dog years or compute their grade point average (GPA). There was little group interaction or discussion as the programs were already outlined in the book, and students merely needed to follow the program guidelines step-by-step in order to re-create them.

Unlike many of the more tech-savvy students who began the course with at least a basic understanding of what programming had to offer and how they might use it in the future, the novice students had little to no computing experience (or in some cases interest), and therefore typically found the class to be extremely boring. To them, they were simply copying a program from a book with no grasp on *why*. We interviewed several students in the programming class who were doing rather well in the course, but who chose not to further pursue computer science study because they felt it had no relation to what they were planning to do in terms of their careers. As one student, Alexa, told us, "I don't think [females] see themselves working on a computer and designing Web sites. I think they see themselves as, like, you know, the doctor, the lawyer type." Evidently, the programming class curriculum did not convey to these students that the problem solving they learn in computer science could be helpful across a variety of careers, nor did it persuade them that computer science might be an interesting subject on its own.

It should be pointed out that it was not just the nontechie students who were disengaged. Indeed, some of the more technically oriented students who began the course with an interest in the subject matter were also disappointed with the class. Pasha, a recent immigrant from the Ukraine, described how his parents bought him a computer when he came to the United States so he could learn how to type and do research. About a year prior to our interview, he got a new, "very good" computer that had "everything on it" and he got interested in graphics. He said it was a lot of fun, and his interest expanded to include everything the computer could do. Explaining why he enrolled in programming, he told us, "I took this class thinking that, why not, you know? If I could take it, why not get a free class to educate me before I try to go into the topic in college?" While the programming course was Pasha's way of testing the waters of computer science and he began with a great deal of enthusiasm, he was left feeling disappointed: "I thought it would be more . . . entertaining. The reason I like the computer idea is because you get away from all the books. It's kind of you and your computer. But we still sit in here with the book. . . . I just wish that we did more, like, projects that we think of instead of more by the book here. Something more creative, you know?"

Pasha touched on a theme that came up with other interviewees as well: the lack of creativity. A good number of programming students explained that what they liked about the computer was that, as one female student put it, "you could be creative with it." And yet the textbook-bound scripted curriculum seemed to squash the creative process, serving as a turnoff for students who might otherwise enjoy computer science and choose to further their study of it.

As at East River, we do not place responsibility for this problematic curriculum solely on any individual teacher. Rather, we highlight these curriculum deficiencies in order to emphasize the fact that the computer science curriculum at the high school level is in desperate need of redesign. In high schools (and colleges), programming is often one of the first computer science classes in the curriculum. The instruction is usually decontextualized from assignments that truly engage students, and is narrowly focused on programming syntax and rote learning (Gal-Ezer and Harel 1998, 1999; Computer Science Teachers Association 2005).[3] As a result, students often come away with a misunderstanding about the problem-solving heart of computer science and uninformed about its larger interdisciplinary applications.[4]

## Computer Science as an Elective "Off to the Side"

The weak programming curriculum is one factor that extinguishes interest in computing, but another is the fact that computer science courses are not central to the academic curriculum. At Canyon this plays out in relation to college preparation. As a school that prides itself on the college-going rates of its graduates, much of what happens at Canyon relates to the college application process. And as competition for university acceptance increases, so does the demand on high school students' schedules. More precisely, in order to make themselves competitive, students are forced to choose classes according to what they believe will provide the most value in the eyes of a college admissions officer.

In California, college-going standards are determined by the University of California admissions criteria (known as A-G requirements). This set of courses is, in essence, a pattern of study designed to assure the college that a student can participate fully in the first-year program at the university in a wide variety of fields of study. Ironically, despite frantic attempts to overhaul education via advanced technologies, and amid cries of panic that the United States is falling behind in its math/science knowledge and not producing enough engineers or computer scientists, computer science is essentially absent from this college preparatory study list. All computer science classes, including programming and AP computer science, are classified as electives only, and only AP computer science counts toward college admissions.

Beyond simply meeting graduation and university requirements, students must also consider whether their classes will add "bonus points" to their GPA, as honors and AP courses do. Likewise, students tend to avoid classes that may put their GPA at risk. Because computer science is perceived as being difficult (in part because it less familiar than, say, AP English), many students opt to take one of the more basic computing courses to fulfill Canyon's technology requirement. This "academic currency" consideration is big at schools like Canyon that have a college preparatory focus, and helps to explain why the AP computer science courses remain insular and dominated by a narrow band of students who are already well versed in the subject matter. Emily, an AP computer science student, notes why there is little drawing power for a broader range of students:

[Computer science] is not one of those big APs like English or calculus or the sciences and stuff like that, or history. I don't even know that most people know about this class. 'Cause, you see there are hundreds of people taking AP English and stuff like that. And this is just . . . well, it's an elective. It's, like, kind of "off to the side." So I don't know if that has anything to do with it. Like, the people who actually take the AP classes are people who know about it and are actually interested in going out of their way to take this.

Student decisions, of course, are not made in a vacuum. While some students shy away from programming or AP computer science for fear of jeopardizing their GPA, or because it does not seem to "buy" them enough, it is often the counselors (and sometimes teachers) who introduce or reinforce these ideas. In this way, counselors and teachers can serve as commodities brokers, pushing certain courses over others because of the perceived value they potentially bring to a student buyer in the college-bound, academic marketplace.

In one of our quarterly meetings with Canyon teachers, a discussion broke out about the hierarchy of AP classes, as viewed by the Canyon counselors.[5] There appeared to be a common understanding—evidenced through the knowing looks and nodding heads of teachers—that certain courses are perceived as more valuable in the college admissions process than others. This applied to even the most subtle distinctions—AP European history, for example, is for some reason (incorrectly) perceived by Canyon counselors as more valuable than AP world history—so given that technology is reflected nowhere in the A-G requirements, and how few counselors have a strong and comprehensive (or even accurate) definition of computer science, it is easy to see why AP computer science holds a lowly position in the AP hierarchy. It also gives us more insight into the ways in which the education system, on both the high school and university levels, plays a role in keeping computer science insular.

### The Insularity of AP Computer Science and "Preparatory Privilege"

One of the biggest challenges in trying to understand why there are so few students of color studying computer science at Canyon is that, well, there are so few students of color studying computer science there. Of course, this limited our subject pool as we set about our quest of uncovering the relationship that underrepresented students had with learning this subject. Yet it was clear that we needed to immerse ourselves in the culture of the AP computer science classroom, despite the fact that the students we were most interested in were noticeably few. We nevertheless hoped that by understanding the paths of students who did find their way into the course, and their experiences taking it, we might gain some new insight about why such a narrow band of students of color was choosing to study computer science. Ironically, it turned out that some of our most valuable insights into the dynamics of course segregation as well as the relationship between underrepresented minority students and technology emerged as a result of a deeper understanding of this course that was so noticeably *absent* of diversity.

Dan, who is white, was excelling in the AP computer science course. He told us that he has three computers in his household, two of which were new. Dan has his own computer (a laptop) and connects to the Internet through a wireless cable network. He loves all things electronic, and planned to attend the University of Illinois and major in engineering (he was undecided on which form of engineering). In describing his love for electronics, Dan put it this way: "I like math a lot. . . . Fiddling around with electronics and all, all types of electronics and technology kind of interest me, you know? I like to take stuff apart and then put it back together."

Ken, another white student, also stood out in the AP computer science class, in part because he was incredibly vocal about his programming talents and had been observed on more than one occasion vehemently arguing with the AP computer science instructor about his grades. His technology interests lay in both video games and animation. On occasion, Ken would stay after class to show his fellow techies his latest updates on an animation piece he was working on, getting input and admiring slaps on the back from his peers. Ken was fortunate enough to have a father who is a programmer, and thus his programming knowledge was rather extensive. Moreover, he had easy access to current equipment and the latest software updates, which helped him to further advance his knowledge and expertise outside of school.

At Canyon, all of the techie students we interviewed came from homes with an amazing wealth of resources that afforded them the freedom to pursue their technology-related interests at leisure and in-depth. In fact, most came into the course already possessing a substantial amount of computing knowledge that allowed them to excel in the class. One techie student, Gene, told us that a number of the students enrolled in the class because they thought it would be easy, fun, and give them an "easy A." While a few of these students had parents who actually worked in the computing industry, others had parents who were engineers or worked in fields that employed similar backgrounds. Those whose parents were not in computer science or related engineering fields at least had parents with the material resources to help further their children's knowledge at home. These students were able to play with their own computers, take them apart, put them back together, try out different software, and learn from friends who were doing the same. In addition to having home access to several computers, students like Dan and Ken had fast and easy access to the Internet, and knowledge of where to go to get the best hardware and software deals. Moreover, many of these students had advanced skills, and were fully capable of not only troubleshooting their computers but also building computers "from scratch." Two students had even created a business assembling equipment and dealing with computer glitches for friends and neighbors.

Because most of these techie students came from the surrounding neighborhood, their friends were close by, and where shared interests existed, knowledge and ideas could be readily exchanged. These students were linked into social networks of other friends who were also acquiring knowledge and experience outside of school; in doing so, they provided each other a peer learning community. These factors cannot be underestimated in sparking, facilitating, and nurturing students' interest in learning more about computing. And as we will see later, the absence of this type of network has an equally powerful—albeit negative—effect. Clearly, the combination of relatively abundant material resources with social networks creates an out-of-school and home advantage—what we refer to as preparatory privilege—that sets up elite students (usually white and, incidentally, usually male) for success in AP computer science.

## The Digital Divide and Contrasting Lived Experiences

In 2006, the National Center for Educational Statistics released the report *Computer and Internet Use by Students in 2003* (DeBell and Chapman 2006), and its findings illuminate much of what we found at Canyon. The research revealed a range of factors, all of which contribute to patterns of computer usage that are clearly split along socioeconomic and racial lines. Only 37 percent of families on the lower end of the income range (in this case, with annual incomes lower than $20,000) use computers at home, compared to 88 percent of families with annual incomes over $75,000. The study also showed that white and Asian students were more likely to use computers at home than were their African American, Latino/a, and American Indian counterparts.

Not surprisingly, and of particular relevance to our research, the study also found that schools were important access and learning sites for students without technology at home. African American students, American Indian students, students with annual family incomes below $35,000, and students from monolingual Spanish households "rely more heavily on access to the Internet from school than on access from any other single location" (DeBell and Chapman 2006, 29). These are the very differences we witnessed at Canyon, and these early access issues are one of the most significant factors in determining early outside experience with technology.

The early access and preparatory privilege of many of Canyon's neighborhood students contrasts with the technology background of many of the school's other students, especially the traveling students of color. It was not unusual for them to report having insufficient technological resources at home, including: out-of-date equipment that could not run necessary software or needed expensive repairs; insufficient access to a computer at home, usually because of the need to share with parents or siblings whose computing tasks might be more urgent; the inability to afford basic software like Microsoft Office Suite or peripheral equipment like a printer; and unreliable, inefficient, or slow access to the Internet.[6]

We are not claiming that *all* students of color at Canyon have minimal technological resources. What we did find, however, was that while the well-resourced techies were predominantly white, *all* the students who reported being technologically underresourced in their households were Latino/a or African American. Canyon does have computers for students to use, but those who are most likely to need them are also less likely to be able to access them—Canyon's traveling students typically cannot stay after school or come early because of their reliance on school bus schedules. Eduardo, a Latino student, observed how these disparities in access affect involvement with computing when he noted that "mainly white kids at this school know a lot about computers." He told us he believes that the white kids have an edge because "during summer, they [white kids] always go to classes," and because they have up-to-date computers at home.

Our research findings at Canyon are in line with national statistics showing that there is still a gap in home access to technology between white families and both African American and Latino/a families.[7] More precisely, our study of Canyon reveals how we have to look more deeply at the digital divide, understanding that equal access is much more complex than the mere presence of a computer in each household. We witness once again the ineffectiveness of well-intentioned policies created without regard for the *lived experiences* of those for whom a policy is intended.

### Demeaning Environment: "Their Work Is a Joke"

At Canyon, all of the computer science courses, including the AP class, are taught by Ms. Carter, a lively and dedicated teacher with a big personality and two teenage children of her own. Though she is a certified teacher, she was also relatively new to the classroom. In addition, the AP Board had recently (in 2004) switched the course's programming language from C++ to Java, giving AP computer science teachers like Carter little time to make the transition. Carter nevertheless has had many years of work experience as a computer programmer and has owned her own software firm, so she offered her students real-world expertise and enthusiasm. We visited Carter's AP computer science classroom over a two-year period, interviewing students, observing classroom dynamics, studying the curriculum, and trying to get a handle on the overall classroom culture. Carter, a committed teacher, was receptive to our research project and willing to help us in any way she could.

During our visits, we found the AP computer science classroom discussions to be routinely dominated by students like Dan and Ken, who came into the course with a firm grasp on much of the subject matter. This happened in the following way, as captured by a summary of our classroom visit field notes:

On this particular day, when Ms. Carter wrote a problem on the board for the class to work through, three to four of the most tech-savvy white male students shouted out possible methods for solving the problem, argued with each other, then got up from their seats and stood in front of the board to discuss the problem, blocking the view from the rest of the class. This classroom discussion then turned into a long private debate among these students and Ms. Carter. The rest of the silent students sat at their desks, listening to the techie students argue while looking at their backs.

To be sure, the eagerness with which the techie students engaged in problem solving at the board was rewarding for Carter, and thus she further encouraged the discussion. She would often enter the fray and ask probing questions, helping to fuel the debate and getting the students at the board to think about alternative ways of solving the problem. Without Carter even realizing it, the end result was that some students engaged in excited argument about a topic they were quite familiar with, while others sat in silence, all but excluded from the conversation. Though the physical blocking of the whiteboard was not necessarily a common occurrence, the reduction of classroom discussion into a private dialogue among the class techies was frequent in our observations, and the consequence was the same.

Although gender dynamics in computer science are not a focus of this book, they were a part of our larger research project, and some of our findings in that area are useful in shedding light on the AP computer science course. For example, female students were the ones who commented the most about these classroom dynamics. Despite impressive backgrounds and parents directly involved in the technology field, the female students commonly described the classroom as male dominated and "intimidating." This was due not just to the usurping of discussions but also to what they perceived to be a demeaning attitude of superiority conveyed by some of their male techie peers. One female student explained how some students would purposefully use code that went beyond what was taught to tackle assignments, simply to show the rest of the class the extent of their "advanced" knowledge. All this perceived "showing off" resulted in an atmosphere wherein some students felt reluctant to ask for help. As Jennifer remarked, "It's a bit intimidating to be in the class when everybody else really thinks they have a strong handle on it. It's all these guys. They seem to know exactly what they're doing, and it's sometimes been difficult even asking for help because I don't [know], really."

It is important to note that the females in the class are not imagining this dynamic. On more than one occasion, our researchers observed the most tech-savvy students rolling their eyes during class discussions, or making snide remarks about what they construed to be their teacher's or classmates' lack of knowledge. This disrespect was thinly veiled. During one interview, a white techie male disparaged the work of two of his non-techie peers, Grace and Ernesto, stating, "Me, Gavin, and Keith, and Bill, we consider them the biggest joke. Their [work] is the biggest joke." He added that when the students were charged with grading each other's assignments, he would share Grace's work with his friends, and they would laugh about it. Facing an environment like that, it is no wonder that so few students without prior experience in computer science feel comfortable in these types of classes.

### Those with "Natural Gifts"

A common theme in our interviews with educators at Canyon was the perception that many traveling students attended elementary and middle schools that did not prepare them for the academic rigors of Canyon. In the context of computer science, this was compounded by the notion—prevalent at Canyon, as it was at Westward—that students who are good at computer science possess some sort of natural gift for the subject matter. At Canyon, the most tech-savvy students enjoy preparatory privilege from home before they even enter the school, and out of view of their fellow students and teachers. And so many of these students who perform well in computer science classes are perceived as having a particular type of smarts, having an inborn gift and desire for computing. A male techie student, Gene, explained that to succeed in computer science, you simply need "pure" thinking. To him, there is no measure of practice that will help one improve, "no trial and error"; instead, "you have to have a good head on your shoulders."

Carter similarly believed that her techie students possessed what she called an "aptitude for computer science," a kind of natural gift that, as one student in our study stated, makes techies "prone to know" computer science. And while Carter acknowledged that effort is important in academic achievement, she also believed that in computer science you either "have it or don't have it." Students were well aware of the fact that Carter holds this notion about natural ability. As Janet, the only African American female to take the AP computer science course, told us: "[Carter] felt if you don't get it, you don't get it, you know? You have to have the mind to do well in this class and just—you get it like that, basically. That's how she was, and she told me plenty of times."

As we know from the previous chapter and as further evidenced here, this belief in inborn qualities can have profound effects on the classroom environment. Here, it results in the propping up of students with preparatory privilege, often leaving other students riddled with insecurity and doubt, and limiting their ideas about what is possible for their own lives.

### "Freedom of Choice" Is Not "Freedom" after All

When they approach me they see . . . everything and anything except me. . . . [This] invisibility . . . occurs because of a peculiar disposition of the eyes.
—Ralph Ellison, *Invisible Man*

Although Canyon offered AP computer science, there were not enough students of color enrolled in this course to talk with us about these critical issues of race. We wanted to hear firsthand from students of color about why they thought the enrollment was low, so we cast a wider net for students to interview. In collaboration with two involved teachers, we were able to hold a series of focus groups with students of color in Canyon's Advancement Via Individual Determination (AVID) and MESA programs.[8] AVID is an in-school academic support program that targets students in the "academic middle," placing them in advanced classes as well as providing academic support to prepare them for college eligibility and success. MESA, as mentioned earlier, is a program whose goal is to increase the numbers of ethnic minority, low-income, and first-generation college-bound students who enter science- or math-based degree programs after high school. The majority of students who participate in these programs are college-bound students of color—the very students we would hope would take advantage of computer science course offerings, but who were noticeably missing. In small group settings, we talked with these students about our research and their views on why the enrollment of students of color so clearly drops as the courses become more advanced. We heard their experiences of being intellectually discounted and disrespected by both teachers and peers in honors classes when they had enrolled, and how they had received inadequate counseling and negative messages about their future prospects. In the process, we learned a great deal about how dramatically and significantly individual choice can be constrained.

It was apparent early on in our focus groups that students have a keen awareness of the role that racial bias plays in shaping the perceptions of students and educators alike, specifically contributing to the notion that "white people are smarter." While many students were quick to point out that it may not necessarily be true that white people are more intelligent than African Americans or Latinos/as, nevertheless, "[people] think it." And this misperception leads to situations that are, to say the least, uncomfortable for students of color, especially in fields such as computer science. For example, Jamie, who is African American, described her experience in her AP classes, such as being discounted by her peers:

They'll condescend to you, like [you are not] as smart as them or something like that. Like you'll ask 'em a question or you'll try to have input on what they're saying . . . [and] they won't really take in what you put in. They won't really use what you said or anything like that. Like if they ask you a question, and you give 'em an answer, they won't really take it as a valid answer or something like that. But if a white kid does . . . they will.

Another student, Keisha, explained what happened to her in her honors English class. She told us how her white peers conveyed surprise over her intellectual abilities and high grades: "I know I'm good in English. That's my favorite subject. I'm really good at it. It's the white kids in that class, when I say something intelligent they look at me in awe, like 'Oh, like that came from you?' And I don't like that."

In her essay "Competing Theories of Group Achievement," Theresa Perry (2003, 97) discusses how "you scarcely can find a Black student who cannot recall or give you a litany of instances when he or she was automatically assumed to be intellectually incompetent." In educational settings, these biased beliefs about the capacity, motivation, and abilities of different racial groups are widespread, and when combined with structural experiences, chip away at underrepresented students' trust, interest, and persistence (Solórzano and Yosso 2000; Solórzano, Ceja, and Yosso 2000; Pierce 1974). In computer science classes, white and Asian students (and males in particular) simply do not have the experience of having their intellectual abilities in the subject doubted solely because of their race or gender.

Many students that we spoke with claimed not to care about such biases, but their other comments revealed something very different. One student's desire to avoid any arena where she will be "watched" or judged, another's conscious "registering" of people's comments about her abilities, and the general open declaration that white people are considered smarter by society at large all indicate that the way other people perceive these students has a profound impact on how they see and interact with the world. In our research, we saw how this constrains the choices they make about whether or not to engage in AP computer science specifically, and the AP pipeline in general.

## Stereotype Threat and the Computer Science Pipeline

Further complicating students' engagement (and disengagement) with certain subjects and the settings they enter are their desires to protect themselves from a phenomenon identified by psychologist Claude Steele (1997) as "stereotype threat." Decades of research on this issue have found how racial and gender stereotypes are often so significant that they essentially become self-fulfilling prophecies, impacting both the degree and quality of participation in different arenas in profound ways.[9] Steele and his colleagues' extensive research on this issue shows how an understandable concern about doing or being anything that even remotely confirms a stereotype can be distracting to the degree that it undermines a student's performance.[10] Ultimately, the stereotype threat can be upsetting enough that a student will disengage altogether from an activity. For students of color who do participate in a "risky" situation, their educational experiences can be vastly different from those of their white peers who share the same classroom space:

Almost every interaction can have that ambiguity to it and the threat to it, the threat that perhaps I'm being treated through that stereotype, so that students, even though they're standing there on the same campus, in the same room with the same teacher, they're really in very different environments. And that's what's been difficult for American educators to appreciate, the difference in those environments.[11]

Our focus group discussions with Canyon students were evidence of how critical it is for computer science educators to consider their schools and classroom environments as the spaces of potential conflict that they are. These psychological vulnerabilities are not minor individual affairs but rather the result of collective actions and history with a wide-reaching impact. Stereotype threat and the role it plays in the creation of what W. E. B. DuBois ([1903] 1989) called "double consciousness," or "this sense of always looking at one's self through the eyes of others," adds a subtle, typically unspoken dynamic to academic decision making: the notion of risk, which significantly complicates our understanding of the very concept of choice.

### Guidance and Choice: How Counselors Reinforce the Divide

As they navigate the sometimes-murky waters of college preparation, students rely on the advice of "experts"—in particular, counselors—to guide them toward their goals, to help them make decisions. This is particularly true for students who do not have a parent who has attended college and therefore require greater input from sources outside the home. Too often, however, counselors (whether intentionally or not) reinforce messages that call into question the academic ability of students of color and their rightful place on an accelerated educational track.

Keisha, who is African American, explained how negative and indifferent messages from educators at Canyon have contributed to her own self-doubt about her abilities, and have largely dictated the classes she takes:

I could be in AP class right now. . . . It's not so much that I'm lazy or anything. It's just . . . I don't have people telling me, "Oh, Keisha, you should do that because you're smart" or whatever. I have people telling me, "Oh, you shouldn't do that. It's too hard," or something like that. I may say that I don't care what people think, but it does register after a while, like maybe I can't do that. So I start to have doubts and then I'm going to take a regular class.

Another student, Jamie, supported this notion, describing how "in black classes, when [counselors] come to the classes that are filled with more minority kids or whatever, they tell them to go to SMC [Santa Monica Community College]," but then when they go to honors classes "they tell you, you can go to UCLA." Jamie painfully and poignantly observed the long-term effects of these messages: "I think, after a long time of hearing that, a lot of people, like, you know, they get scared of the Advanced Placement. They don't feel that they belong. Like they're probably SMC material instead of, like, UCLA material."

In general, most of the students in our focus groups felt that the role that counselors played in college planning was at best nebulous, focusing more on filling schedules than on strategic planning. Students reported needing to investigate classes on their own so they could tell their counselors what they wanted and then hope for available space. This conversation with David, a student enrolled in the programming course, illustrates the point:

*Interviewer:* How are your course decisions made?

*David:* A counselor.

*Interviewer:* You meet with the counselor regularly?

*David:* No, he just . . . every six months or whenever the semester's over, he comes by and says, "OK, you need to fill this requirement and your period four's open, so would you like to take this class?"

*Interviewer:* So no one has sat down and talked with you about your interests?

*David:* No, you are probably the first person, besides my mom or something.

Research on counseling practices in schools with high numbers of students of color confirms David's perceptions. As we discussed in the previous chapter, although counselors are a vital source of information when it comes to academic planning and college choices, in many instances their caseloads are simply too large and their responsibilities are simply too diverse to allow them to offer college counseling effectively (Hugo 2004; T. K. Miller 1998; Monson and Brown 1985). Canyon, for example, has roughly 2,700 students and only 4 counselors, making the student to counselor ratio about 675:1. It is virtually impossible for the counselors to get to know all the students well enough to guide them toward optimal academic schedules. Thus, when they do "help" students shape their academic schedules, they rely on parameters such as the University of California's A–G requirements, which as we have already discussed, automatically preclude the importance of enrolling in computer science. And in the case of Jamie's observation, the counselors may rely too heavily on assumptions and biased beliefs, and too little on real information about their students' abilities and interests.

The ineffectiveness of college counseling at the high school level is especially problematic for students of color. Research shows that because these students are more likely to be the first in their families to attend college, they are also more likely than their white counterparts to be influenced by their school counselors when it comes to their academic futures (Lee and Ekstrom 1987; Plank and Jordan 2001). Unfortunately, counselors may be less likely to place these students in college preparatory classes (Atkinson, Jennings, and Livingston 1990), and historically have not encouraged students of color to pursue postsecondary education (Lareau and Horvat 1999; Perez 2000). The cumulative effect of this multitude of shorter-term decisions can easily be extracted from research on de-tracking, which examines what happens when students who have constantly been chan-neled into lower-level courses are suddenly given the freedom to enroll in whatever classes they please, including upper-level, honors classes. In short, they often do not go. Messages about students' capabilities become so ingrained that it appears nearly impossible for students to make choices outside of these "leveled expectations": "educators and their peers had told them for many years where they did and did not belong within the hierarchical spaces of their schools," and tragically, "over time, the stu-dents' recognition that they occupy a low-status place" becomes part of who they are (Yonezawa, Wells, and Serna 2002, 52).

### Classroom Interaction and Isolation

Counselors and the courses to which they guide their students are not the only influences on students' aspirations. Teachers are also in incredible positions of power when it comes to influencing the ways that students see themselves. Our interview with Janet, the only African American fe-male who was enrolled in AP computer science during the course of our study, illustrates the power of teachers' attitudes and comments, and the subtle and not-so-subtle ways that they can impact students' lives. Janet enrolled in AP computer science because she thought it would be inter-esting and enjoyable. The curriculum was different from what she had expected, and as a result, she struggled with the material. Nevertheless, Janet felt she had to persist: "I think it was mainly because we [African American females] were so limited in the world, you know, and just be-ing able to be in a class where I can represent who I am and my culture, I think, was really important to me. And so I think that was really the main thing that kept me there."

Janet noted that despite the fact that many of the students were expe-riencing difficulty with the concepts (and eventually, about half the class dropped the course), she was the only one who was approached by the teacher, Carter, about how she was faring in the class. Carter, who later told us that she was worried about how the class would affect Janet's overall GPA, pulled her aside and in a quiet but public conversation dur-ing class, suggested to Janet that she drop AP computer science, adding that she should not feel bad because some people just do not have "the aptitude" for this kind of study.

Admittedly, the concepts in the course were difficult and new to Janet, but just as crucial, the hard drive in her home computer had broken and this led her to have problems completing the assignments. Despite the teacher's intention to help her, and despite Janet's own knowledge that there were extenuating circumstances, what she ingested from the conversation was the impression that her teacher felt she did not have the necessary talent and was not smart enough to handle the work. Moreover, she felt humiliated in front of her peers.

One of the more painful lessons we learned through this project was just how, well, *painful* it can be for students of color to be isolated on the accelerated track. The decision to enroll in these courses, when no other students of color are enrolled, requires an enormous amount of psychological risk. It is therefore easy to see why some students choose to stay in "regular" classes, where they have more friendship groups and support networks. It can be difficult, if not impossible, to break into the social networks that have been formed (in some cases) over a lifetime. So, for example, it did not surprise us to hear Keisha (who was introduced earlier) tell us that in her mostly white honors class, she did not "really talk to anybody" because the other students were "kind of standoffish when you try to talk to them." The isolation that students like Keisha felt in their accelerated classes was for many enough to tip the scales away from the honors track; ultimately, what became painfully apparent from the focus group discussions was that having so few African Americans or Latinos/as in advanced classes leaves students of color who do enroll feeling marginalized, unsupported, and alone.

These feelings are well supported in the literature. In *Talking about Leaving*, for instance, researchers Elaine Seymour and Nancy Hewitt (1997) found that college students of color who were in the minority in science, mathematics, and engineering majors experienced the same type of isolation. They wondered if others judged them as incompetent, experienced doubt that they belonged, held back from seeking help or asking questions, and were miserably lonely without peer groups with whom to share their experiences. The result was that students often moved to majors where they would be less isolated. It became obvious to us that a similar dynamic exists at Canyon, and as such, that too many students of color choose to stay away from the AP/honors environment altogether, enrolling instead in classes where their friends are, in order to feel supported and avoid the constant feeling that their abilities are being called into question.

### The Posse Effect: Breaking the Isolation, Breaking the Pattern

Perhaps one of the biggest lessons we learned from Canyon was the extreme importance of social networks, both in the acquisition of knowledge and learning how to move forward in a field, be it computer science or academia in general. These networks can include counselors or teachers who might encourage a particular path of study, and parents or family members who can demystify the subject matter for students, and in some cases, offer a base of knowledge and support. And then there are friends. Young people look to each other for cues on what clothes to wear, what music to listen to, which classes to take, and which to avoid. Peer networks can play a vital role in helping students emerge from the margins, from the shallow end, to pursue their academic interests. And in the absence of these supports, students are left to fend for themselves, often with misinformation or no information at all.

The data from our focus groups and interviews supported this notion. One Latina student, for example, said she consistently earned As, but because no one had ever suggested to her that she should move to an accelerated, honors track, she stayed on the regular course. An African American male in the same focus group said he did not start taking honors courses until he joined AVID, simply because up until that point, he was unaware of the advantages they afforded him. One of our more disturbing findings was that some of the African American and Latino/a students we interviewed actively chose to stay in regular-tracked classes because they thought that the high grades they were earning would give them an advantage in terms of college competitiveness. What was not conveyed to many of these students was the weight that college admissions officials place on honors and AP classes. And in the absence of mentors or a network of peers to tell them otherwise, these students' misguided notions persisted.

While social networks are ubiquitous among the middle classes, and provide vital paths to privilege and opportunity for them, students of color typically experience the opposite—"that is, the ubiquity of network barriers and entrapments" (Stanton-Salazar 1997) along with the resulting absence of an informed, active network is limiting, to say the least. It is not surprising, then, that building networks is the cornerstone of many effective programs at the college level that are directed at supporting underrepresented students. Sometimes referred to as building "critical mass" or the "posse effect," these initiatives are based on the importance of supportive communities (residential and nonresidential) where students in the underrepresented groups can reinforce each other's learning and offer support for one another.[12]

The story of one Canyon student, Jennifer, makes it clear that change can also come directly from the students themselves. The strategy of this determined AP computer science student offered us valuable insight into at least one approach that is feasible for promoting change in a school such as Canyon. Jennifer took Canyon's programming class at the urging of her father, who runs a Web-based business out of their garage. Jennifer works part-time for her father, and he suggested that a programming class might help her to better understand the data-mining programs they use, thus allowing her to be more efficient at her work. She enjoyed studying programming because of what she called the "challenge" of it and the fact that it was "logic driven." While she really enjoyed the subject and wanted to continue her computer science studies, she had no interest in persisting in what she felt was an unfriendly and somewhat exclusive environment. While Jennifer is white, and her concerns had more to do with gender than with race, but there are still critical lessons to be learned from her story because they speak to issues of exclusivity and isolation: What Jennifer did not like about programming was the male-dominated culture of the classroom, and she found the environment to be intimidating at times, making it difficult to ask for help.

So when she decided to enroll for a second year, she called her friends. Jennifer touted the benefits of a computer science education to her female friends, telling them what she liked about it and reminding them of the weighted grades they would receive as a result of taking an AP course. Ultimately, she also asked them to enroll with her so that she would not be the only female taking the class, so that they could serve as a support system for each other within this homogeneous, male-dominated environment. That year, 2002–3, three females enrolled in AP computer science: Jennifer and two of her friends. While this is an embarrassingly small number, it is important to keep in mind that it is a 200 percent increase over female enrollment from the prior year. The following school year, six female students enrolled, reflecting a 200 percent increase over the 2002–3 school year and a 500 percent increase over the 2001–2 school year.

Jennifer, it seems, found a way to protect herself. Intent on further pursuing her computer science studies, but also knowing it would be difficult to tolerate another year of feeling intimidated and isolated, she brought her own support network with her the second time around. And it made a big difference. Jennifer told us that with friends and a greater understanding of the material going in, "I feel like I can participate in conversations more than I could before, 'cause last year, I found myself really quiet. I isolated myself 'cause I didn't know anything, and everyone else seemed to know what they were talking about." With an expanded support system comprised of students who she felt were similar to her, Jennifer began to feel that she belonged in the class, and that allowed her to pursue computer science further. The story of the girls' posse in AP computer science is particularly compelling because it points to the key role of social networks, and eventually critical mass, in shifting the dynamics of classroom environments and allowing all students to access a full range of resources as well as advantages as they prepare for their futures. It offers us a glimpse into one of the ways that change must be effected for students of color.

### Breaking the Isolation

In the end, the dynamics at Canyon forced us to reexamine our understanding of choice and what it means for students of color to choose. We learned how students' decisions to enroll in particular subjects of study are shaped by multiple forces, and are not simply a matter of personal interests or desires. Most students, it seems, make these choices based on a cost-benefit model, but the factors they must consider vary significantly. The predominantly white AP students who know how to navigate the academic sphere tend to make choices that will reap the most academic reward on the path toward college. In essence, the same is true for Latinos/a and African American students. Yet the difference is that they are often denied the necessary resources to guide and prepare them, and they must also face the psychological burden of racialized conspicuousness, constantly reinforced negative stereotypes, and painful isolation—all of which (understandably) can lead to disengagement with a field and more advanced courses of study.

In his article "Race and the Schooling of Black Americans," Claude Steele (1992, 77) discusses how for underrepresented students, the building of a respectful relationship between teacher and student should be "the first order of business—at all levels of schooling. No tactic of instruction, no matter how ingenious, can succeed without it." All students, but especially students of color and females in white- and male-dominated subjects, need to perceive that their teachers value them for their academic potential and as people. In fact, these relationships are one of the most critical components in building trust and reducing students' sense of vulnerability. Indeed, our focus groups also revealed how much students of color at Canyon "hungered for 'places of respect'—classrooms where they were not racially isolated and their cultural backgrounds were valued" (Yonezawa, Wells, and Serna 2002, 40). This is particularly pertinent for fields such as computer science where the underrepresentation is acute and the isolation is frequently extreme.

Taken together, our series of three school portraits allows for a comparison of circumstance. At East River, we saw how students of color are systematically denied access to computer science courses because such classes do not even exist. The organizational constraints are simply too great and the pervasive stereotypes too strong—and so computer science essentially falls off the map. We saw more of the same at Westward. Through student and teacher comments, we gained an even greater understanding of how a sorting process takes hold—with students of color stuck in the shallow end—and becomes integral to "what is," with no thought to whether the effects are malleable, proper, or even just. And finally, at Canyon, we continued to see many of these same historical inequalities and biases play out, but now in a vastly different context— one where resources are *more* plentiful, and the curriculum is relatively *stronger.*

As we traveled the metropolitan area of Los Angeles, visiting three different schools, looking through a narrow lens of computer science education, we discovered how the underrepresentation in computer science cannot be understood in isolation; it is intricately tied to the state of U.S. schooling, and is further linked to how schools educate (or don't educate) students of color. Toward the end of our research we were faced with the question, What now? What do we do with this information? That is the subject of our next chapter.

# 5

## Teachers as Potential Change Agents: Balancing Equity Reform and Systemic Change

Toward the end of our research, we were at a crossroads: we faced the question of whether to act on what we had learned up to this point or continue doing more research. With the question "What next?" ever present in our minds, we concluded that we could not just walk away, write our research papers, and be done with the situation. We had witnessed the large disparities in educational opportunities and felt we were in a position to galvanize the necessary resources to do *something*. One of our team members, Joanna Goode, had been an AP computer science teacher in a large urban high school for several years and knew firsthand how teachers needed support to do their jobs right. Another team member, Jane Margolis, had been involved in a project of institutional change at the university level, and had experienced the results of alliance building around gender and computer science (Margolis and Fisher 2002). Together, we were all committed to doing the same around race. So taking our combined expertise, and informed by the findings of our research project, we launched an equity reform initiative focused on teachers' professional development—offering the support teachers need to do their jobs well, and engaging teachers with efforts to broaden participation in computing.

In this chapter, we discuss a summer institute we initiated for LAUSD computer science teachers and the promising results and complex outcomes that occurred over a short time. Our model was to help build the capacity within LAUSD to broaden the participation in computing. Our first initiative was to create an opportunity for teachers to acquire the necessary content and pedagogical tools they needed to teach computer science. But we added another component as well. We wanted to begin a process so that teachers could become change agents. Here we discuss the results that ensued, but also the deep-seated challenges that continue to threaten the improvements that resulted. Specifically, this type of work requires thinking about what teachers need to do their jobs well, yet it also requires thinking about the political pressures bearing down on the schools—the realities of urban schooling that shape every element of teaching and learning. This chapter is ultimately about a tense balancing act that inevitably occurs as reformers straddle that line between the practical and the political, between equity reform and deep systemic change.

## Teachers Are Key

As those of us who have had an influential educator in our lives realize, the care of a teacher can have a lasting impact on a student's life interests and pursuits (Goode 2007, 65). In fact, one of the most influential resources for increasing students' opportunities to learn and raising their achievement levels is access to qualified teachers (Darling-Hammond 1997, 1998). And yet preparing and supporting computer science teachers is one of the largest dilemmas within computer science education (Goode 2007; Computer Science Teachers Association 2006). Training and professional development opportunities for computer science educators are sorely lacking; at times this may be the primary obstacle to creating high-level courses. Indeed, at the time of our research, only twelve of the fifty-seven LAUSD high schools offered AP computer science classes, and not having the right teacher was cited as one of the major reasons. Few teacher education programs offer methods courses for computer science teachers, creating no clear pathway for becoming a teacher in the discipline (Computer Science Teachers Association 2006).

Throughout our research, we encountered countless well-intentioned, talented educators with some basic computing training who did not have access to the knowledge and resources required to present a more academic, relevant computer science curriculum to students. Beyond strict content issues, teachers in the computer science classroom also have a burning need for engaging pedagogical techniques that make computer science exciting and meaningful for a diverse body of students. And while the ever-changing, technology-driven nature of the discipline and the complex interdisciplinary connections make computer science as exciting as it is, they also make the task of developing a curriculum even more challenging, especially for educators who lack any specialized training. When you place all of these issues in the larger context of schooling, where computer science teachers are extremely isolated, it is clear that urban computer science teachers do not have the necessary professional development and community to support their work. Further, as so conclusively shown by our research, teachers need a computer science curriculum and the support of their district leaders, principals, and counselors for their efforts directed at broadening the participation in computing.

## The UCLA/LAUSD Summer AP Computer Science Teachers' Institute

Toward the end of our research, in 2004, we launched the Computer Science Equity Alliance (CSEA), an interdisciplinary K–20 partnership, with a mission of helping to build the capacity of LAUSD teachers to teach computer science and broaden participation in computing. We formed an institute around a critical K–12 and university partnership model, knowing that the expertise of both institutions must be involved in this task. CSEA consisted of three interdisciplinary partners: ourselves from education, Dean Vijay Dhir from the UCLA Henry Samueli School of Engineering and Applied Sciences, and Dr. Todd Ullah, representing several LAUSD divisions.[1] The years of collaboration and a trusting relationship between Ullah and us were the foundation that allowed this program to develop as it did. The goals of the teachers' institute were as follows:

- To help teachers teach Java (the programming language of the AP exam)
- To explore an engaging computer science pedagogy—one that is meaningful for urban youths
- To create a community of practice for LAUSD computer science teachers where teachers can learn from each other as well as share ideas and information
- To provide demonstrations and insights into the current interdisciplinary applications of computer science
- To engage teachers with the equity issues involved in computer science education, devising strategies to support them and their work around broadening the participation in computing

The LAUSD led the effort in recruiting teachers for the institute, and each LAUSD high school principal was invited to send a potential AP computer science teacher. In total, twenty-five teachers from twenty-two schools enrolled in the first pilot teachers' institute in 2004.

## The First Compromise: Focusing on AP Computer Science

In line with our overall mission of increasing access to and engagement with computer science learning for students of color, the first *practical* decision we had to make was which group of teachers would we gear the institute to. We decided on current and potential AP computer science teachers with the hope that more AP computer science teachers with up-to-date professional development would result in more AP computer science courses in the district, especially in schools with high numbers of students of color. Focusing on AP computer science was not an easy decision for us to make, for we have serious criticisms of this specific course and the AP system in general. AP courses tend to teach to the test, and as a result, the content can often be a mile wide and an inch deep. In terms of AP computer science specifically, we were concerned with the almost-exclusive focus on programming. The narrowly defined AP computer science course neglects other topics that constitute the breadth of the computer science discipline, making it not representative of the larger computing discipline. Further, the course (like many other upper-level mathematics and science courses) has historically served only a narrow group of white and Asian students.

In the LAUSD, the lack of diversity in AP computer science reflects the national and statewide trend of predominantly white and Asian male enrollment.[2] Figure 5.1 shows the dramatic underrepresentation of African Americans, Latino/as, and females, and the proportionate overrepresentation of whites and Asians taking the AP computer science exam in California. Though these percentages mirror general nationwide trends, the underrepresentation of Latino/as is much more severe in California than the national average. Across all states, Latino/as represent 16 percent of the high school student population and 6 percent of exam participants. In California, however, Latino/as represent 41 percent of the high school population but only 8 percent of the exam takers. The same severe underrepresentation of Latino/as was present in LAUSD classrooms at the time we began our first partnership initiatives in 2004. Though 69 percent of the LAUSD high school population is Latino/a, only 24 percent of the students enrolled in AP computer science were Latino/a.

Despite our sharp criticisms, we chose to focus on AP computer science in this case for strategic reasons. First, at this time, AP computer science is the only computing course in California that counts toward college entry requirements; it is thus a more rigorous course and is arguably the only one in a position to attract college-going students. Furthermore, because of a recent court case (*Daniel v. State of California*, 1999) suing the state of California for the lack of AP courses in overcrowded schools, we expected, and found, district leaders to be more supportive of our initiatives, as they were eager to increase the presence of AP in the

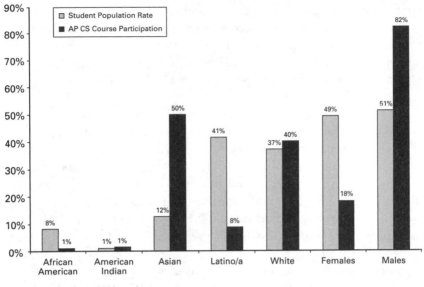

**Figure 5.1**
Comparison of California student population and California AP computer science participation by demographic group, 2004

*Note*: Sample size = 2,788 students.

*Sources*: National Center for Educational Statistics (2004); College Entrance Examination Board (2004).

LAUSD schools. And of course, we were motivated by the understanding that students cannot enroll in courses that do not exist; they also cannot engage with courses that are not engaging. With that in mind, we set out to both increase the number of AP computer science courses that are being taught in the LAUSD and improve the quality of instruction.

## At the Teachers' Institute: Broadening the Vision of Computer Science

The two weeks of the summer institute included intensive Java instruction combined with discussions about the broader issues of computer science instruction and equity issues. We emphasized the importance of highlighting computer science topics other than programming as a way of hooking students (and teachers) into studying computer science. We arranged for teachers to visit several UCLA computer science laboratories, which demonstrated cutting-edge computer science research and applications for them. The teachers watched software mimicking precise human movement with the effect of gravity, witnessed the use of interactive set props in the theater department, followed a robot around a room, and observed environmental scientists collecting data using censors with attached radios. They also had opportunities to converse with UCLA professors and graduate students.

We focused on equity issues too, sharing our research with the teachers, engaging them in discussions about how to think about a broader group of students who could potentially be interested in learning computer science, and describing how to make assignments and the teaching of computer science more meaningful and relevant, connected to their surrounding communities and the students they teach.[3]

Too often—particularly in subjects that are thought to be objective, like computer science—classroom practices can be disconnected from students' lives, seemingly devoid of real-life relevance. Not only is it important for computer science teachers to show that there are computer scientists who "look like" their students, it is also vital that they communicate the fact that computer science is relevant. But computer science teachers have typically not had assistance or support in developing these types of approaches—approaches that allow them to demonstrate the significance of the subject matter to students and their communities—especially at the high school level, and this needs to change.[4]

The work of Eric Gutstein (2001, 2007) in mathematics is a useful example of this kind of tailoring. Gutstein (2007) describes assignments such as asking students to read articles about Latino/a population growth, and then use percentages and graphs to answer questions about it; having students learn about mathematical and economic principles through media coverage of farmworkers' wages; requiring students to analyze SAT data—disaggregated by race, gender, and income level—and then write letters to the Educational Testing Service about their findings; and providing students with mortgage rejection rate data and asking them to determine whether race plays a factor. These are all examples of ways in which so-called objective material can be grounded in issues that matter to the students who are learning it. And thinking back to our descriptions of computer science courses in our three schools, this is unfortunately not the way that computer science is typically being taught. We began to explore the need for resource development in the institute and intend to address this more as we continue to work with LAUSD teachers.

One of the pedagogical challenges we faced during the institute was that the teacher participants had a broad range of educational and professional backgrounds. Of the participants in the first year, only four held undergraduate degrees in computer science. The other teachers majored in mathematics (four) or business (seven) in college, and others received degrees in fields such as English literature, music, and Spanish.[5] Professionally, participants had been in the classroom between one and twenty-five years. Two of the teachers had taught AP computer science for more than a decade and were well versed in the curriculum, one teacher had begun teaching AP computer science two years prior, but most teachers had not previously seen the AP computer science curriculum. Given this range of knowledge and experience, differentiating instruction for teachers with different skill levels was essential during the instructional components of the institute. Ironically, this "uneven development" model is what often happens in many high school classes, so we used this as an opportunity to reflect on this pedagogical challenge that teachers face when they are in their own classrooms. The institute began in 2004 and has been held every summer since, so as to continue supporting the work of veteran and new LAUSD computer science teachers.[6]

## Our First Result: Finding Gold

Because the LAUSD was in charge of recruiting teachers to the institute, and principals were involved in this process, teachers were identified to attend the institute who we likely would not have met in other ways. The first result of this institute, then, was what we refer to as "finding gold"— finding a diverse set of teachers who had been in their schools wanting to teach computer science, but had not been able to do so because computer science was not being offered.

Mr. Landa, for example, is a Latino University of California at Berkeley graduate in computer science who was teaching mathematics in a large, all-Latino/a East Los Angeles high school. He had long wanted to teach computer science, and not until our institute launched this district-sponsored program was the principal willing to start up a new course in the school. Landa began teaching it at his school, and later, when he moved to a brand-new school in the same neighborhood, he integrated a set of three new computing courses in the school curriculum. In 2006–7, his AP computer science class enrolled thirty-two Latino/a students.

Another teacher involved in the institute also developed a series of courses in computer science at his high school. Mr. Palomares, a teacher in one of the district's low-performing schools, had a core group of students very interested in technology and was looking for the opportunity to start a computer science academy within his larger school complex. As we write, that academy has just been launched.

Like Landa, Ms. Pai also has an extensive background in computer science and was eager to teach computer science at her low-performing school, yet she did not have the opportunity until the district-supported institute. Pai, born and educated in India, has a master's degree in computer science from Mangalore University and was teaching in a public high school in Watts, a low-income area of Los Angeles. Never before had the school offered AP computer science. Through the summer institute, Pai became involved with efforts to change that, and was particularly committed to recruiting more females to her course in the poor, all-minority school.

Ms. Olear, originally from Nigeria, currently teaches at a high school that is 70 percent Latino/a. She has a BS in mathematics and an MA in education from Pepperdine University. Olear began her teaching career as a mathematics teacher, but after receiving an announcement about our summer institute, her principal (who knew about her programming background) asked her to attend and teach AP computer science in her school. Since her first year of teaching the course, she has made tremendous increases in the diversity of the students.

There were numerous other remarkable teachers who also participated and made great strides at their schools, and this was the beginning of one of the most important accomplishments of the institute—the identification and training of a diverse group of dedicated teachers who could now teach computer science.

## The Need for School-Level Institutional Support

Knowing that teachers would need institutional support to keep the classes scheduled, interested students enrolled (rather than dumped), and resources available, following the second summer teachers' institute in November 2005, we organized a daylong seminar at UCLA with LAUSD district officials, principals, counselors, teachers, and university computer science educators. Over fifty educators attended, among them principals, assistant principals, teachers, mathematics coaches, MESA coordinators, magnet coordinators, counselors, and district leaders. We discussed the lack of diversity in computer science nationwide, its significance as a new high-status knowledge, the current disparities in course opportunities that exist in the district, the need for teacher professional development, and the need for institutional support from counselors and other support teachers. Chris Stephenson of the Computer Science Teachers Association and Jan Cuny of the NSF's Broadening Participation in Computing division were invited to address the LAUSD educators to give the larger national perspective.

We had learned how important this "buy in" was from the principals after the first pilot institute in 2004. That first year of the institute, we had invited the participants' principals and counselors to attend on the last day so that we could talk with them about the crucial work their AP computer science teachers were engaged with, and why this work was key both locally and nationally. Yet after this first summer institute, when the teachers returned to school, not all of them found the course on the master schedule. Clearly, we needed to develop more understanding and commitment on the part of the administrators. Our LAUSD partners responded immediately to this, and for the following years of the institute (2005 and 2006), each principal was provided with more information and a contract committing them to scheduling AP computer science for the following academic year if a teacher attended the institute.

### A Model Program Developed for Students and Teachers

As institute participants embarked on teaching AP computer science, they found the content of the course challenging for students and quickly expressed the need for additional support for their students, who typically had no school-site tutoring or additional learning support at home. We responded to the call from teachers for extra instructional support by organizing monthly, Saturday computer science sessions at UCLA in which teachers and students attend computer science enrichment lessons. This program, called AP Computer Science Readiness, was built off a pre-existing outreach program created to supplement AP mathematics and science instruction in the LAUSD.[7] Still operational after three years, each year the AP Computer Science Readiness program attracts about forty to fifty AP computer science students and eight to ten teachers. Most of these students are students of color who come from low-resourced schools, and about one-third of the students who attend are females.

These devoted students and teachers are transported to the UCLA campus via school buses, often getting picked up as early as 6:30 a.m. on a Saturday morning; they typically don't return home until late afternoon. The ongoing monthly participation of students and teachers in a rigorous university outreach program serves as an important counternarrative to the belief that "kids are lazy and don't care about education."[8]

At AP Computer Science Readiness Saturday sessions, the UCLA computer science department provides a computer lab and classroom space for the computer science program so that students are immersed in a college-level environment. David Smallberg, an exceptional UCLA lecturer, teaches these sessions along with Joanna Goode and different LAUSD teachers; as a result, students receive a taste of authentic, high-quality, college-level instruction. The sessions provide students with challenging AP computer science computing problems, AP test preparation, and education/career information about computer science, and they offer teachers with the opportunity to observe university instructors and their own teaching colleagues as they lead lessons—a rare opportunity for high school teachers in any field. Additionally, lecture notes, curricular materials, and question-and-answer sessions all benefit the professional development of teachers. This monthly time together has been beneficial for the participating students and has also become a de facto space for informal LAUSD computer science department meetings where relevant topics are addressed among the community of teachers. This allows them to share pertinent information as they strengthen their vital social network.

The AP Computer Science Readiness program is a key component of our efforts to institutionalize and sustain these reforms within the district. In contrast to many professional development initiatives that sweep in from the outside for a one-time session, our attempt has focused on fostering teacher leaders within the schools, building collaborations between K–12 and the university, developing a program that can help support students, and building the capacity of schools with high numbers of students of color to offer and sustain rigorous learning opportunities.

## Building a Learning Community of Computer Science Teachers

After the first year teaching AP computer science it was clear that some teachers needed additional, focused professional development. Moreover, other potential computer science teachers were interested in joining the effort. Almost annual changes in the AP computer science course—

whether a language change, case study change, or course audit, for example—require ongoing professional development programs. These constant changes in curriculum can overwhelm teachers and drive them away from teaching AP computer science, making this type of continuing support absolutely essential. In response, as an extension of the institute, during the year we provided "support on demand" to the teaching community. For instance, we offered two support sessions to help teachers with the College Board's recent audit process.[9] An even larger issue involved curriculum.[10] In the absence of a viable curriculum for teaching AP computer science, UCLA researchers collaborated with the LAUSD to purchase a respected AP computer science curriculum for all AP computer science teachers. The quick response to the curricular needs of teachers helped establish increased trust between district officials, university researchers, and classroom teachers.

Besides these types of supports, one of the most important developments was the formation of a computer science teachers' community. Computer science teachers are traditionally isolated in their schools, with no collegial support in the planning and teaching of computer science. There is typically no computer science department within high schools, so computing teachers belong to various other departments, such as business or math. Before this teachers' institute, computer science teachers rarely had the opportunity to interact with other computing teachers from other schools. One of the accomplishments of the CSEA has been the creation of an ongoing space for computer science teachers to share ideas, learn from one another, and develop professional networks. Through the summer institute and activities throughout the year (for example, our AP Computer Science Readiness program), our efforts went beyond a "one-shot deal" and instead contributed to the creation of a consistent, ongoing community of practice for computer science teachers within one district.

This community also made it possible for teachers to share their best practices. For instance, in the first year after the institute, Olear was disappointed with the small AP computer science class size and the lack of diversity. Despite the diverse nature of the majority-Latino/a school, she had mostly white and Asian students, and all boys, enrolled in the course. So Olear, in response to the CSEA goals, developed a strategic recruiting plan to remedy this situation for the next cohort of students: The spring of her first year teaching AP computer science, she designed a flyer about the course and gave a lunchtime presentation for students interested in taking an AP class. She introduced herself, described the course, explained the benefits of studying computer science, and answered questions. Her presentation included diverse images and emphasized the non-nerd applications. Olear left a letter for each student personally inviting them to enroll in the course. As a consequence, in a single year, her enrollment increased from twelve to sixty students—a 400 percent increase. Amazingly, her female enrollment also increased from zero to twenty girls. When Olear shared her approach with colleagues, there was excitement among the other computer science educators about the possibility of this approach at their own schools.

**A Remarkable and Rapid Two Years of Results**

The results following two years (2004 and 2005) of the summer institute and AP Readiness program were remarkable and rapid. In the academic year prior to the first institute (2003–4), out of 57 LAUSD high schools, only 12 offered AP computer science, and only 225 students studied AP computer science in these 12 schools.[11] The year after the first institute (2004–5), 22 schools offered the course and 395 LAUSD students were studying AP computer science; the following year (2005–6), 23 schools offered the course and 619 students were studying AP computer science—over two and a half times as many students as before the intervention. Not only did enrollment increase during this time but traditionally underrepresented groups also had the largest gains. Latino/as *quadrupled* their enrollment and females *tripled* their enrollment. Figure 5.2 below displays the increases by ethnic and gender groups. We must note that African American students nearly doubled their participation, but this increase is not on par with overall enrollment, and therefore we still see room for improvement. The overall district enrollment, though, is particularly remarkable considering it occurred during a period when California participation in AP computer science courses decreased by 17 percent.

**The Continuing Challenges**

Despite CSEA accomplishments, there have been a series of political challenges that emanate from the state of urban schools; these challenges are then compounded by the confusion around computer science education in particular. As we know from our case studies, computer science is

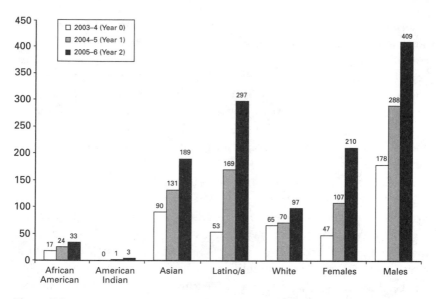

**Figure 5.2**
AP computer science enrollment increases over three years in the LAUSD by demographic group
*Source*: Data courtesy of LAUSD Information Technology Division, School Information Branch.

extremely vulnerable to broader influences such as overcrowding, not enough classrooms, revolving administrations, shortages of textbooks and other curricular materials, the formal and de facto tracking of students, the lack of a college-going culture within schools, testing pressures, high numbers of underprepared teachers (especially mathematics and science teachers), high numbers of English-language learners, the lack of academic supports for students, the shortage of counselors, and the lack of student guidance. In addition, AP computer science teachers must not only continue to learn the changing topics of computer science content and develop an engaging pedagogy, but they often are also without computer lab technicians, and are responsible for loading software and maintaining computers that may or may not work in the first place.

Unlike most other college-required subjects, where teachers have colleagues at their local site, computer science teachers frequently are the only ones teaching the subject at their school. As such, they must contend with all of these issues in relative isolation. They also face the additional tasks of attracting and recruiting students, especially traditionally underrepresented students (i.e., students of color and girls), and educating counselors about the importance of identifying potentially interested students to computer science in the first place. Their classes are often further complicated by the phenomenon of "double rostering," which happens when a course does not fill to capacity (as regularly happens with computer science), and so two or more different courses are assigned to the same teacher simultaneously. For instance, a teacher might be assigned a geometry course with twenty students and an AP computer science course with fifteen students in the same class period. The extra energy and time that teachers must devote to teach one period of AP computer science is a tremendous obligation that can negatively impact their attention to their other courses. These are the factors that challenge even the most dedicated teachers' commitment, and put the teaching of computer science at peril on a yearly basis. One teacher, who is a certified mathematics instructor, told us that her preparatory time for AP computer science is more than double what it is for a mathematics class. She has been teaching AP computer science only because of her commitment to the goals of CSEA, and whether she will continue is questionable at this time. Sadly, hers is not the only story of frustration and setbacks.

### One Step Forward, Two Steps Back

The story of a talented LAUSD AP computer science teacher who had been actively involved with our summer institute presents a sobering reminder of why computer science education is always at risk in these types of low-resourced and undersupported schools, and how even in light of the remarkable increases in students taking AP computer science across the district, there remains work to be done. We already mentioned Pai, who was teaching in the public high school in Watts, a low-income area of Los Angeles. Never before had the school offered AP computer science. Pai became very involved through the summer institute, and was particularly committed to recruiting more females to her course in the poor, all-minority school.

Pai's first year of teaching AP computer science was a tremendous success. She was a talented teacher, creating a community of inspired and active learners in her class. In the year following the institute, there were fourteen Latinas, two Latinos, and four African American males enrolled in her AP computer science class. Considering that only nineteen Latinas took the AP computer science exam the prior year in the entire state, this diverse course enrollment was impressive. The following year, however, the principal canceled the course. State tests identified this school as scoring in the lowest decile in mathematics and language arts, and the continued underperformance kept the school in program improvement status. (As part of the No Child Left Behind program, a school is put on notice for improvement before being taken over by the state.) Pai, who was a certified mathematics teacher in a school that was short of certified mathematics teachers, was moved from computer science to more mathematics instruction. AP computer science became a casualty and another example of the triage decision- making that regularly occurs in low-performing schools. This was a great loss for our program and, more important, for the students at this school who were interested in, and for the first time had the opportunity to enroll in, AP computer science.

The story of another teacher, Mr. Ramirez, who attended our institute right after he began his teaching career, again demonstrates the toll of urban schooling.[12] Ramirez had graduated as a mathematics major from UCLA with a specialization in computing, and had recently obtained his master's degree in education. Ramirez began his teaching career at a brand-new South Los Angeles high school serving Latino/a and African American students, and was hired because of his computer science background. Committed to working with traditionally underserved populations, Ramirez launched an AP computer science course during his second year teaching and recruited thirty students. Yet despite the districtwide efforts, he was largely unsupported at his school site. For instance, Ramirez was given no assistance in maintaining a computer lab—a considerable burden for a new teacher.

But Ramirez's critique of schooling conditions went far beyond the computer lab, as he described to us the existing challenges of providing quality core mathematics courses at his school. A glance at the state test results reveals a horrifying statistic: on the California standards test, only 1 percent of students scored at or above proficiency in mathematics at this school. With four mathematics courses and only one AP computer science course on his schedule, Ramirez felt unable to maintain the effort required to teach this AP computer science class in addition to his other teaching responsibilities. Given this, after much consideration he decided to commit his efforts toward overhauling and streamlining the mathematics course sequence at his school.

Ramirez's dilemma is the same one we heard repeatedly from principals and administrators, and we wrestle with it ourselves all the time: if students' mathematics proficiency in the district is at such a low level, where should a teacher like Ramirez put his time and energy? It is essential to remember that this dilemma is a daily event in one form or another at low-resourced schools. This "logic of scarcity" constantly shapes decisions and conundrums such as Ramirez's; educators like him in similar schools are left feeling that something must be sacrificed because there is not enough to go around. And the end result is that interested students who could benefit from taking more rigorous courses, such as AP computer science and others, are being denied access.

Ultimately, these types of decisions that teachers and principals must make, especially as the No Child Left Behind testing pressures have mounted (as we will discuss in the next chapter), have meant that the outreach efforts have been more difficult to implement in the lowest performing schools in the district. We have been especially thwarted in those high schools with a majority of African American students, and this is a challenge that we are committed to addressing.[13]

**Where We Are Today: The Need for Engaging Curricula**

As our research has clearly shown, the computer science pipeline must be studied and addressed within the whole schooling context. What this ends up meaning is that reform in one subject, in the context of urban schooling, will commonly be stymied by conditions in the schools that continuously undercut the best of intentions. And in turn, even the most basic of equity reforms are impacted and often undercut by local and national politics that are usually out of touch with the realities of teaching and learning in urban schools. In short, the obstacles are multilayered.

For these reasons, many computer science curricular reformers have focused their energy outside of urban schools. They have galvanized more around informal, outside-of-school programs, figuring that they can do more good and reach more kids if they circumvent schools like the ones we have described. There are thus some innovative and effective informal educational programs through organizations like the Girl Scouts, Computer Club Houses, and computer summer camps (to name a few), and many of these are innovative programs that reach large numbers of youths.[14] But we remain committed to serving the students who populate urban schools *within* their schools, for these are students who are frequently unable to participate in these informal opportunities or attend more well-off schools because of location, financial resources, or other access issues. So our choice is to focus at the school level, developing teacher leaders and offering the supports we can to students who become involved in these classes. We find ourselves having to be *strategic* as we try to do our best navigating the numerous obstacles. Many times we have felt that we are compromising in ways that were not comfortable (such as focusing solely on AP computer science). But the alternative was to not take any *practical* action at all, and after our time in these schools, that simply was not an option.

Toward the end of these three years of working with teachers and students, our funding was dwindling and the LAUSD was in financial and political turmoil. Given this, for the last year and a half, we have been able to offer only "emergency" support to teachers, and have not been able to follow up on the outcomes for the students.[15] Despite the continuation of our professional development and outreach programs, CSEA almost fell apart due to a gap between grant awards. We found ourselves treading water so we could continue our partnership work with the LAUSD.

As we conclude this book, we have recently been notified of funding support to continue our efforts.[16] Our work will still be based on a university-K–12 partnership, offering professional development for teachers and student support; but we will now be thinking beyond AP computer science, initiating efforts to design an alternative and engaging computer science curriculum along with an innovative sequence of courses within the LAUSD, all with the goal of institutionalizing and sustaining these reforms aimed at increasing access to computer science learning for students of color.[17] A critical component will be outreach work with principals and other policymakers in the district. These are the "gatekeepers"—the ones best positioned to change the culture of their schools—who must understand our program is part of a larger effort to assure that rigorous, college preparatory curriculum is an integral part of schools with high numbers of students of color.

We will continue our work with teachers, now focusing on their potential as change agents and teacher leaders. In an article on this issue, University of Toronto professor emeritus Michael Fullan (1993) notes that though many teachers enter the field with a moral purpose of wanting to teach and help children, they are missing the skills of change agentry, and as a result, many burn out and get discouraged. The capacities to become effective agents of change are not developed individually but must be nurtured and consciously shaped collaboratively in a professional setting.[18] Our current vision, then, is one that will create an innovative computer science course that qualifies for university admissions, establish understanding among school administrators about the importance of our work, while helping to build the capacity of LAUSD computer science teachers so that higher-level learning opportunities will have a chance of being established, especially in schools with high numbers of students of color. Our vision is "one that works simultaneously on individual and institutional development" (Fullan 1993, 12). We agree that "one cannot wait for the other," to cite Fullan (3; see also Goode 2007).

### Developments across the Country

All across the country, there are interdisciplinary and cross-institutional teams of educators and organizations working with teachers, and focused on broadening the participation in computing. Most notably, organizations such as the Computer Science Teachers Association, the National Center for Women in Technology, and multiple projects in the NSF's Broadening Participation in Computing program are working tirelessly and creatively on this issue.[19] Industry, too, has been initiating K–12 support programs.[20]

A notable endeavor that has been designed to enhance professional development for computer science teachers as well as change state policy as it pertains to computer science instruction is the Georgia Computes! project.[21] Its biggest effect has been from the partnership between the Georgia Institute of Technology and the Department of Education, which together in 2004 created the Institute for Computing Education (ICE). The goals of ICE are to increase the quantity and quality of Georgia computing teachers, and the quantity and diversity of computing students in Georgia. To this end, ICE offers teacher workshops during the summer and throughout the school year. A representative of Georgia Computes! (Barbara Ericson) has also served on the committee that revised Georgia's computing curriculum, so that it is now based on the Association for Computing Machinery's Model Curriculum for K–12. This curriculum has been adopted by Georgia and is being put into practice so that more teachers are now seeking computer science training. A representative of Georgia Computes! also served on the committee that created a computer science endorsement to supplement the teaching credentials of Georgia's educators. In addition to teacher training and policy work, Georgia Computes! has run successful summer camps and collaborative workshops for parents and kids.

Georgia is not alone in its efforts to broaden participation in computer science on a state level. Concerned about the low numbers of students entering computer science in state universities, South Carolina has recently formed the Computing Competitiveness Council to advocate for computer science education in high schools. This collaboration of computer science faculty, education faculty, high school teachers, parents, and industry has received support from the state superintendent of schools. Spearheaded by Dr. Duncan Buell of the University of South Carolina, the council is focusing on many of the same computer science issues as the Georgia project. First, though there is a computer science graduation requirement in South Carolina high schools, this requirement is typically met through computer literacy courses, not computing classes. In fact, only 219 South Carolina students participated in the AP computer science exam in 2007. The council aims to work with schools to provide curricular guidance in developing a more rigorous course to satisfy this graduation requirement, while simultaneously expanding access to AP computer science. It has begun to pilot this work in a large, urban high school. Second, the council is committed to pursuing computer science teacher certification for South Carolina teachers so there is a clear path for computer science majors to teach in high schools. It will also offer summer professional development opportunities for teachers. All of these efforts, including our own, are partnered with the Computer Science Teachers Association, an organization that is committed to issues of equity and broadening participation in computing to include a more diverse group of students.

## The Practical and the Political

As we have worked to support teachers as leaders and change agents, we have found ourselves continually struggling with the tension between the practical requirements (such as helping teachers find a better curriculum, providing teachers with professional development, and building supports for students) and the overarching political context of urban schooling, knowing full well that much larger forces must be tackled in order for true equity to occur. We live with this tension every day, and have not completely resolved it to our satisfaction. We have certainly learned that there are no quick fixes.[22] Rather, a constellation of factors must be simultaneously addressed when engaging in this type of equity work in urban schools. What may appear to be a simple solution to the "outside world," and what perhaps would be a relatively easy reform in a well-funded suburban school, is not simple at all in a large, overcrowded, urban district. While we are aware that it may be easier to work outside of a large school system—and all of its inherent dysfunction—to focus our energies elsewhere, we have not done so. Our hope is that this chapter and book will help in "translating" some of the issues confronting computer science education in urban schools so that more university/K–12 partnerships can flourish.

# 6

## Technology Policy Illusions

As we were studying our three schools, we became increasingly alarmed by the seemingly manic ways in which the simple provision of technology has been offered as the prime solution to what is, ultimately, a larger and more complex problem of educational inequity—a problem that is both systemic and deeply rooted. We do not mean to dismiss out of hand the numerous initiatives that are directed at bringing up-to-date technology into schools. Access to technology is essential, and we value the ways in which computers can spread enthusiasm among students, the ways that technology can enhance students' ability to access and process information, and how that can and has changed the nature of teaching as well as learning. But our research has made it clear that any effort to assure that all students have access to the high-status learning of computer *science* and other such subjects will require more than a personal computer and a modem. It will require policies that provide students with a sequence of powerful learning opportunities, quality teachers, and student support systems. It will necessitate policies that look at the whole educational system, and address the interactions between structural inequalities and belief systems so prevalent in the schools. And it will demand policies that help build the capacities of the schools and are based on a true understanding of the complicated realities of schooling. While policymakers have hoped for technology to be the "great equalizer," the profound segregation and inequality that continue to exist throughout our educational system have not been altered. In many cases technology has contributed to even further inequities. Our three case studies are examples of this.[1] Nevertheless, it is important to understand the broader policy context from which these efforts have emerged.

### The Origins of Technology Policy

Over the last two decades, policymakers have been devoted to closing the digital divide in high schools by increasing funds to purchase computers, getting schools wired, and integrating technology throughout the curriculum. These policy initiatives contain explicit and implicit assumptions about the benefits of technology to students, teachers, and schools. Such policy assumptions range from the curricular (that technology enhances student engagement with learning, and that it helps teachers create better lessons), to notions about the fundamental relationship between access to computers and life chances for students (Culp, Honey, and Mandinach 2003). Indeed, the most pervasive presumption threading through these policy initiatives is the idea that giving low-income students access to computers and integrating computers into course work will not simply increase student achievement—thereby leveling the academic playing field—but also provide students with critical job skills for the high-tech economy. In this way, policymakers have viewed technology as an educational *and* social magic bullet—a quick and straightforward way to create both educational and social equity (Light 2001; Oppenheimer 2004).

The origins of the recent policy push for technology education in schools can be traced to the National Commission on Excellence in Education (1983) report, *A Nation at Risk* (Culp, Honey, and Mandinach 2003). This report declared that the U.S. educational system had fallen into such a state of disrepair that the decline amounted to a state of "educational disarmament"—and it concluded that part of the problem lay in the fact that students did not have the technology skills that the new economy would require of them. The report found that the academic deficiencies documented in U.S. students "come at a time when the demand for highly skilled workers in new fields is accelerating rapidly." The opening paragraph of *A Nation at Risk* argues that our "once unchallenged preeminence in commerce, industry, science, and technological innovation is being overtaken by competitors throughout the world." It goes on to claim that even though we can be proud of our educational system, "the educational foundations of our society are presently being eroded by a rising tide of mediocrity that threatens our very future as a Nation and a people."[2] The report points to technology as a likely solution, contending the following:

• Computers and computer-controlled equipment are penetrating every aspect of our lives—homes, factories, and offices

• One estimate indicates that by the turn of the century, millions of jobs will involve laser technology and robotics
• Technology is radically transforming a host of other occupations, including health care, medical science, energy production, food processing, construction, and the building, repair, and maintenance of sophisticated scientific, educational, military, and industrial equipment

The accompanying push for increasing technology in education was premised not just on the needs of our national economy but also on the assumption that increasing students' access to technology would lead to greater social equity. As the report noted, "The people of the United States need to know that individuals in our society who do not possess the levels of skill, literacy, and training essential to this new era will be effectively disenfranchised, not simply from the material rewards that accompany competent performance, but also from the chance to participate fully in our national life." It concluded with a number of recommendations, including that high school graduation requirements cover the "new basics" at the core of the modern curriculum: English, mathematics, science, social studies, and computer science.[3] This new emphasis on the need to train students in computing sparked a massive reaction by policymakers, who spent the ensuing decades trying to get computers into schools and to get schools wired. Since 1993, U.S. schools have spent over "$40 billion in infrastructure, professional development and technical support" (Dickard 2003, as cited in Culp, Honey, and Mandinach 2003).

Local and state technology initiatives have echoed many of these assumptions about the relationship between technology, achievement, and social equity. For example, California's Digital High School technology grant program, enacted in 1997, allocated funds over four years to supply computers and Internet access to California's high schools. The program aimed to provide "all high school students with basic computer skills" and "to improve academic achievement in all subject areas" (Schiff and Solomon 1999). The Digital High School legislation itself states that:

1. Computer knowledge and skills are essential for individual success in school and career, and for the continued economic prosperity of the state of California
2. All pupils in California must be "computer literate" before they complete high school
3. Traditional learning is enhanced by appropriate technology.[4]

Taken at face value, these goals and principles are simple and straightforward. But as our research has shown, there is another aspect of technology policy that goes beyond the provision of equipment and is anything but straightforward: it shows how policy has failed to address pressing equity questions— specifically, which students are learning what types of technology *knowledge*, and what implications do *disparities in learning opportunities* have for the individual students? Technology policies have been successful at increasing the number and quality of computers in schools serving low-income students, but they have not addressed the underlying distribution of knowledge that different students are receiving. When one identifies which students are going beyond learning basic computer literacy skills, critical gaps are revealed—gaps that leave students from different backgrounds prepared for very different futures.

## The Illusions of Technology

In an analysis of the history and origins of technology public policy, Northwestern University professor Jennifer Light (2001) discusses how the framing of the digital divide as a question of access to computers reduces this incredibly complex issue to an oversimplified technological solution. Broad coalitions of groups from businesses to education, including groups that would normally disagree with one another, joined the call to wire up schools and other public institutions to assure access to computers. But in doing so, interest groups across the political spectrum "turned attention away from how other structural forces that create problems of inequality continue to exert their effects" (711).

Light explains how policymakers have historically latched on to technological fixes, even though physical artifacts in the schools do not solve the equity gaps. For instance, educators in the 1970s and 1980s had high hopes that the performance gap in mathematics would be closed when hand calculators were provided for underachieving students (Light 2001, 714). Yet access to calculators did nothing at all to change the achievement gap.[5] A similar flurry of hope and activities surrounded the installation of cable television in the schools, but as Light argues, technology simply will not solve the problems of students who have been unprepared, stuck in schools with low levels of resources, unqualified teachers, and inadequate learning opportunities. Light captures the illusions associated with technology: "It is comforting to imagine that the diffusion and use of a particular technology will remedy complex social problems.

Hopes for a more equal society are one of the most popular fantasies fastened onto new technologies" (716).

Given these hopes, it is no surprise that Digital High Schools, new media academies, and laptop programs are popping up all across the country, as educators cling to the belief that technology, finally, will hold the key to achieving a state of educational parity.

### Different Skills, Different Destinies

Maine is home to one of the first and most ambitious technology programs, where all middle schools and a growing number of high schools provide laptops for all of their students.[6] Committed, dedicated, and visionary educators at both the local and national level are associated with this initiative. Although relatively few studies evaluating the laptop program in Maine have been conducted to date, those that have been done found the program to be positively received by students and teachers, in part because it seemed to help increase student engagement.[7] Still, hardly any of these studies have sufficiently addressed the larger equity issues and the disparities in learning opportunities that continue to plague low-resourced schools.

A series of studies being led by Professor Mark Warschauer at the University of California at Irvine does speak to these equity issues. In 2006, Warschauer and his team completed a study called "Laptops and Literacy," in which they surveyed ten schools over a two-year period, focusing on literacy and learning challenges in the context of laptop programs in both high- and low-SES schools (Warschauer, 2006a, forthcoming). They found that laptop computers contributed to increased collaboration and student engagement with literary processes, but that the inequality gap between the achievements of the high- and low-SES students was not narrowed. While benefits such as increased engagement, increased access, and demonstrated enthusiasm from parents did accrue for the low-SES students, the researchers also found that there were countervailing forces that resulted in low-SES students and the schools that served them often being less prepared to take advantage of the full capacities of the laptops (Warschauer 2006a, 26). For instance, in the high-SES schools, the entire community including the library, counseling department, teaching staff, and plenty of parent volunteers were there to help integrate the laptops into the instructional program that already had a strong focus on student research. In contrast, the low-SES schools struggled to attract top-notch teachers, administrators, and staff. Further, there was much less of an emphasis on developing research skills at those schools, and students were praised for simply citing online information without regard to its content or source, or for producing low-level PowerPoint presentations that involved little more than cutting and pasting from the Internet (Warschauer 2006a, 28).

Warschauer's earlier studies also point to the same set of problems, highlighting how different groups of students are being prepared unequally for their futures, with students in low-SES schools getting the lower-level preparation. Studying technology access and use in eight California high schools, his team found that while the low-SES schools had a slightly better student-to-computer ratio on average than the high-SES schools, there continued to be a greater emphasis on using technology for research and analysis in the high-SES schools, whereas in the low-SES ones technology was used simply for display (such as PowerPoint presentations) or more cut-and-paste activities like typing and replication (Warschauer, Knobel, and Stone 2004). In a different study of technology's role in two schools—one low- and one high-SES school—Warschauer (2000, 5) observed that "one school was producing scholars and the other workers. And, the introduction of computers did absolutely nothing to change this dynamic, rather, it reinforced it."

As shown in table 6.1, data from the U.S. Bureau of Labor Statistics illustrates how students entering technology jobs with lower-level computing skills will qualify only for relatively lower-paying and lower-status occupations. As we can see from this list of the most prominent technology jobs, and the skills and educational levels required for them, it is the highest-status computing knowledge—computer science and computer engineering—that is most financially rewarded in the job market today. While jobs at the lower end of the pay scale, such as Web designers, desktop publishers, and data entry, are growing tremendously, the wages they pay hover around the mean U.S. per capita income level, which in 2006 was $39,140 according to Bureau of Labor Statistics (2006).[8]

These data, when viewed in the context of our research findings, illustrate how students from low-resourced schools experience education that leaves them qualified, at best, for only the relatively lower-paying jobs (i.e., the types of jobs that society expects them to engage in as adults), whereas students from more resourced schools (and middle- to upper-class families) have the opportunities to pursue an education that

**Table 6.1**
Job growth, skills, and rewards

| Job | Education required | Job outlook | Mean annual earnings in 2006 |
| --- | --- | --- | --- |
| Computer scientist | Master's or doctoral degree | Increase *much faster than average* for all occupations | $96,440 |
| Computer software engineer | At least a bachelor's degree | Projected to be *one of the fastest-growing* occupations over the 2004–2014 period | $87,250 |
| Computer programmer | Bachelor's degrees commonly required | Growth expected to be *much slower than that of other computer specialists* | $69,500 |
| Database administrator | Bachelor's degrees commonly required | Growth expected to be *much faster than the average* for all occupations | $67,460 |
| Network and computer systems administrator | Bachelor's degrees commonly required | Growth expected to be *much faster than the average* for all occupations | $65,260 |
| Web publication graphic designer | Bachelor's degrees commonly required | Growth expected to grow about *as fast as average* for all occupations | $43,830 |
| Desktop publisher | No college required, though high school diploma preferred | Growth expected to *increase faster than the average* for all occupations | $36,120 |
| Data entry and information processing | High school diploma | These jobs are expected to *decline* | $25,640 |

*Source*: U.S. Bureau of Labor Statistics (2006)

will train them for the top of the occupational ladder.[9] Research that has examined these issues on a broader scale confirms this inequity pattern.

The 1998 "Teaching, Learning, and Computing Survey" studied the relationship between teachers' use of computer technology, their pedagogies, and school contexts across *hundreds* of schools (Becker 2000). This study found that while students in low-SES secondary schools often used computers more frequently than their affluent peers, their use was limited to vocational and remedial tasks. In contrast, students in high-SES secondary schools were more likely to use computers for more academic purposes, such as simulations and research. The study also showed that teacher pedagogy and expectations for students played a large role in the ways students interacted with technology; and as we have seen, these factors can be problematic, even at the most resourced schools, because they limit students' engagement and creativity in such vital ways. As Warschauer (2004, 585) points out, technology can thus become another inequity within and between schools, and that "technology does not exist outside of a social structure, exerting an independent force on it, but rather that the technological and social realms are highly intertwined and continuously co-create each other in myriad ways."

Recently, *Education Week*, a weekly news journal for educators, included a review of the last ten years of technology in schools. One of the lead articles, "Getting Up to Speed" (Trotter 2007), begins with a descriptive portrait of technology in schools today: most classrooms have multiple, multimedia computers linked to the Internet, and "teachers have the tools that those in many other professions enjoy, and many receive training to hone their use of technology in instruction"; the article sums up these advances as ones where "American policy leaders can take a bow" because "most schools today have technology for learning that few imagined just a decade ago." Yet this review is also a critique, pointing to evidence that all the new technology has not translated into great leaps forward in students' learning, and that few U.S. schools are "making optimal use" of the technology tools they have received. In fact, as cited in this review, measured by reading, mathematics, and science scores on the federally sponsored National Assessment of Educational Progress, the average student achievement is little better than it was ten years ago (10).

This lack of progress can be traced to the fact that in the flurry of getting computers into the schools, policymakers have been noticeably silent about what students should learn to do on computers, or what skills would provide students with the presumed educational and social benefits outlined in the technology policies. At a basic level, most of the technology initiatives are predicated on the notion that simply putting students in front of a computer and getting them "computer literate" will offer educational as well as social benefits.[10] While computer literacy skills are absolutely necessary, these initiatives do not acknowledge the limitations of learning only the bare minimum. And they certainly do not address the larger disparities in learning that occur within and between schools, or the fact that students in low-resourced schools are being denied an avenue out of the shallow end of learning. We therefore concur with Light (2001, 717) that initiatives like these, which bring computers into schools and homes, arguably filling people with hope, are often more attractive to specific stakeholders because they are "far less threatening to the status quo than government-sponsored desegregation or other policies designed to attack inequality."

## No Child Left Behind: Narrowing the Curriculum

The question of who is learning what types of technology knowledge becomes even more poignant when understood in the context of broader educational policy and change. Increasingly, students of color are more likely to face a "stripped down" and narrowed curriculum across the board, owing to an overemphasis on testing and accountability that places greater importance on test scores than on real learning. Stanford University professor Linda Darling-Hammond (2007a, 2007b), one of the country's leading experts on teacher quality and educational reform, discusses how the 2001 No Child Left Behind initiative has forced teachers to teach to the test, and as a result, schools have adopted scripted, test-prep curriculum rather than the creative, problem-solving thinking skills required for the twenty-first century.[11] Issues like an overemphasis on testing outcomes are certainly not new, but sweeping reforms like No Child Left Behind that are focused almost exclusively on test scores certainly aggravate the situation (Meir and Wood 2004).

The Bush administration's 2004 National Education Technology Plan touts technology as a "transforming" tool, with claims that by harnessing technology, we can expand access to learning and close the achievement gap. Indeed, the report is titled "Toward a New Golden Age in American Education: How the Internet, the Law, and Today's Students Are Revolutionizing Expectations."[12] Toward this end, No Child Left Behind included a requirement that all eighth graders—from all racial and ethnic backgrounds—be proficient in the "use of technology" by 2005, along with an Educational Technology State Grants Program that awards nearly $700 million in formula grants to states to assist schools in meeting this goal. Yet technology proficiency at the local level has typically been aimed at a rudimentary level, as witnessed by the LAUSD's computer literacy graduation requirements.[13]

As we have already discussed, we recognize the inherent value of technological skill as a stepping-stone to the vast majority of careers that await high school students when they graduate. At the same time, however, we believe that the very opportunity to study computer science—in a meaningful way, beyond simple cut-and-paste, rudimentary lessons—is symbolic of broader educational opportunities. Our schools should offer students courses of study that introduce them to higher-order thinking and problem solving, and challenge them with rigorous content. Students at all schools, regardless of the demographics of the student population or the level of financial resources available, should have the chance to explore diverse subject matter that equips them to make informed decisions about their educational and occupational futures. In fact, in addition to the current emphasis on technology in educational reform, there is also a push to provide higher-level learning to a broader range of students. But the question remains, Is it working?

## A New Convergence: Worry about the United States Losing Its Competitive Edge

U.S. policymakers are in a panic about U.S. innovation and competitive standing in the world. As a result, there has been a flurry of directives aimed at increasing focus and resources for improving science, technology, engineering, and math education, especially at the precollege level.[14] The White House launched the 2006 American Competitiveness Initiative, with its focus on new federal support to improve the quality of science, technology, engineering, and match education in our K–12 schools, and programs to "engage every child in rigorous courses that teach important analytical, technical and problem-solving skills."[15] *Tough Choices or Tough Times*, issued by the New Commission on the Skills for the American Workforce (2006), focuses on the critical links between problem solving, critical thinking, abstraction, and interdisciplinary knowledge for the new job requirements in our twenty-first-century world. The report argues that "the core problem is that our education and training systems were built for another era, an era in which most workers needed only a rudimentary education," and therefore our education system must be transformed. It goes on to describe the nature of these new jobs, pointing to the pervasiveness of technology in almost every aspect of work:

Routine work is largely done by machines in a world in which mathematical reasoning will be no less important than math facts, in which line workers who cannot contribute to the design of the products they are fabricating may be as obsolete as the last model of that product, in which auto mechanics will have to figure out what to do when the many computers in the cars they are working on do not function as they were designed to function. (7)

While it is true that higher-order skills are required in higher-level jobs in the twenty-first century, it is also essential to recognize that the push to provide them is not a new phenomenon. University of California at Berkeley professor W. Norton Grubb (2007), in an essay titled "Life after High School: Taking the Education Gospel Seriously," defines the "education gospel" as the belief that "schooling focused on preparation of the labor force can solve virtually all social and individual problems." Grubb argues that the higher-order skills being promoted are right, but "they aren't especially new, of course, since these capacities have always been taught in the upper tracks of high schools and in the best universities; they are competencies necessary for professional and managerial occupations, and are surely valuable in other employment"; he continues with the observation that "if there's anything new, it's the suggestion that they should be extended to all students" (Grubb 2007, 33). Therein lies the challenging but critical task to which our work is devoted.

While policymakers are pronouncing that twenty-first-century jobs require a much more highly educated workforce, this declared imperative is being undercut by the current focus of reforms emanating from No Child Left Behind. Our study of computer science is an example of this. Grubb acknowledges that the attempt of No Child Left Behind to address the achievement gap is a crucial goal, yet he predicts how "the threatened extension of NCLB testing to high schools would only reinforce drill-oriented remediation and would have disastrous effects on completion" (Grubb 2007, 33). Case in point: many states use new high school exit examinations, tests that students are required to pass to obtain a high school diploma, for NCLB accountability. A study conducted by the Center on Education Policy (Zabala and Minnici 2007) examined two school districts and found that the "emphasis on exit exam preparation may be detracting from other instructional experiences," because, for example, students have less time available to study longer pieces of literature, go into topics in more depth, or take electives. This study also found that in one of the districts "in the schools that served greater numbers of lower-performing students, lower-income students, and students of color, teachers reported that the TAKS [exit exams] had influenced every aspect of the curriculum." Whereas "in the school that served greater numbers of higher-performing students, higher-income students, and white students, teachers reported that TAKS has exerted a less invasive influence on curriculum" (4).[16] And so just as we witnessed at East River and Westward, this narrowing of the curriculum is especially true and onerous for low-resourced schools with high numbers of students of color.

As we write, Jonathan Kozol, author of *The Shame of the Nation* (2006) and *Savage Inequalities* (1992), has been on a partial hunger strike to protest the demeaning of curriculum that is occurring because of the No Child Left Behind law. In an interview with *Newsweek* (Tyre 2007), Kozol describes the devastating impact that reauthorizing No Child Left Behind will have:

Black and Hispanic children are being handed a stripped-down, debased curriculum. They are being trained to provide predictable answers and that provides a terrible danger for a democratic society. Principals, so terrified of No Child Left Behind and determined to pump up the scores, are restricting students' learning to mechanistic skills in a narrow range of subjects. This does not equate to learning. And we see that, for all the obsessive drilling, any gains that supporters of No Child Left Behind claim are there are not being sustained.

Our study of high school computer science leads us to the same conclusion.

### Technical, Normative, and Political Dimensions

Technology policy turns out to be an example of how many ambitious policy efforts are "stymied by the tensions between policy makers' straightforward imperatives for schools to do differently and do better and the conditions which prevent schools from accomplishing their goals" (Oakes and Wells 1997). The conditions, though, are not simple. They are multilayered, and are deeply embedded in our institutions and psyches. They include critical institutional constraints (so-called technical issues such as the shortage of teachers and the need for curriculum improvement), but they also go beyond the walls of the school, and include the normative and political forces within our society that undercut reform efforts (Oakes and Rogers 2006).[17]

The normative forces that thwart school reform are the deep-seated cultural beliefs and assumptions that bolster existing school practices. These are the notions about what types of students can succeed in higher-level learning, about different competencies belonging to different ethnic groups, and about low expectations for students of color that we witnessed at all three schools in our study, and they are seemingly held by almost everyone at the school site—including classroom teachers, counselors, principals, and district officials who make school policy and resource decisions. Policy efforts to increase the number of underrepresented students of color learning computer science in particular, or enrolled in higher-level learning more generally, must create a venue for educators to examine and deconstruct these conventional assumptions, for it is these misguided beliefs that end up as the rationalization and justification for the achievement gap as well as the disparities in learning opportunities between different schools.

There are also political dimensions that must be addressed. Specifically, the pressures of global capitalism to reduce the cost of labor and shrink investment in the public sector hover over all schooling, and influence decisions about and within the classroom. We have witnessed a continuous slashing of investment in our nation's social structures, justified through mainstream political beliefs that our government and its institutions are too big, and thus we must "starve the beast." Increasingly, however, good jobs (and middle-class lives) demand more and more education, and as a result, more powerful middle- to upper-class families exert their power to improve their own schools. Less well-off families, who have historically wielded less political power and leverage, are then left with the poorest of the schools, and the disparity is rationalized with the "logic of scarcity" that has permeated almost all public policy. This logic is a lie, as witnessed in California, where the lack of qualified teachers, the lack of courses, and the overcrowded schools cannot be attributed to limited resources; in a state with among the highest per capita income rates in the nation, this is simply not an excuse (Oakes and Rogers 2006, 158–161). Nevertheless, the logic of scarcity is rampant, and has heightened the competition for advantage in education, resulted in unequal distribution of funds for schools, and further undermined prospects for equity.

The authors of the article "Software Entrepreneurship among the Urban Poor: Could Bill Gates Have Succeeded If He Were Black? . . . or Impoverished?" (Amsden and Collins 1999, 216) poignantly address how decades of technology policy in the schools have *ignored* these broader dynamics at the expense of students of color and students from low socioeconomic backgrounds:

Quick fixes—like the dumping of computers into inner-city schools—may encourage the necessary tinkering with hardware that seems to flow in the veins of software engineers. But such gestures are far from sufficient to ensure even a small, steady stream of inner-city entrepreneurial talent. Even before that flow can start to trickle, imbalances must first be addressed in the state of education in general, computer education in particular, job training and job availability, and other factors that currently serve to make real levels of human capital so disparate among different economic classes in the United States.

Reformers for equity must be working on all three fronts—technical, normative, and political—to help build capacity in the schools. Unfortunately, as we have described, most educational policy has been narrowly focused on technical solutions, and has not addressed the normative influences and the larger political forces bearing down on the entire system. Likewise, teachers are often blamed for broader systemic problems, accountability measures are put in place without adequate funding to help build the capacity needed to meet the goals without sacrificing in other areas, and policies are designed by policymakers, many of whom remain insulated from the realities of schooling and do not understand anything about the complexities of the educational environment. This is not to say that there is nothing to do short of major systemic change. There is plenty. Yet we wholeheartedly concur with the Computer Science Teachers Association (2005, 15) white paper that so astutely warns, "Change is a long-term process, not a short term intervention."

## Computer Science in a Larger Context Again

Currently, all around the country, there are efforts being launched to broaden participation in computing, to increase the numbers of traditionally underrepresented students studying this field.[18] But as our research has shown, underrepresentation in computer science cannot be studied in isolation from larger schooling dynamics, because what we have discovered about computer science is also reflected in other areas of schooling. In California, high schools that are majority white or that have at least a significant white student population tend to have more advanced courses (such as advanced mathematics and AP classes), while predominantly African American and Latino/a schools as well as schools

**Table 6.2**
California high school course availability along lines of class and race

|  | Percent of schools offering computer literacy course | Percent of schools offering AP computer science course |
|---|---|---|
| High-poverty schools | 45.2% | 5.2% |
| Low-poverty schools | 22.7% | 16.2% |
| High-minority schools | 43.2% | 6.1% |
| Low-minority schools | 35.4% | 11.8% |

*Note*: For this analysis, California high schools were sorted into quartiles based on the socioeconomic and racial makeup of students. The lowest and highest quartile by SES and race was compared for this analysis. Statewide, there are a total of 57,965 students enrolled in computer literacy, and 2,654 students enrolled in AP computer science.

with high numbers of English-language learners receive fewer physical and educational resources (including qualified teachers, adequate facilities, and curricular resources), and enroll significantly fewer students in AP classes (Brown 2004; University of California Accord 2006; Zarate and Pachon 2006).[19] An examination of learning opportunities in California high schools demonstrates these unequal opportunities in the computer science discipline (Goode 2007). As table 6.2 shows, students attending high-minority and high-poverty schools are more likely to be offered computer literacy courses; students attending low-minority and low-poverty schools are more likely to have access to AP computer science classes.

These pervasive educational disparities ultimately mean that more students of color are less prepared for college and a full range of occupational choices. Indeed, for every hundred of California's Latino/a, African American, and American Indian students who were ninth graders in 2000, only fifteen graduated from high school having passed the courses required for admission to the California State University or University of California systems. This is half the rate of whites (thirty for every one hundred), and one-third the rate of Asians (fifty for every one hundred) (University of California Accord 2006, iii). So it is not at all surprising that when we asked Sara, an intermediate algebra student at East River, what her image of a computer scientist was, she told us this: "I'd probably see a lot of white people working on the computers. I don't know why. [Latinos] just don't go to college, 'cause a lot of Latinos, they just don't go. A lot more white people and more Asian people go to college and universities."

Unfortunately, Sara is right. The underrepresentation in computer science is clearly a systemic problem that requires a strategy larger than one computer, one subject, or one school. It requires systemic change, which must happen on multiple fronts. It requires the interdisciplinary expertise and social influence of higher education in partnership with K–12, and a movement of teachers, students, and parents who insist that no student will be stuck in the shallow end.

# Conclusion

## "The Best and the Brightest"?

In this country, we are raised on the American dream. We want to believe that anyone can be anything they set their mind to, and this dream permeates all of our beliefs and institutions, including education. Basic K–12 education is what we provide to everyone, no matter what their family's social station, and education is mythologized as the means by which anyone can rise out of current circumstances and reach for any star. President Bill Clinton put it this way: "If you work hard and play by the rules, you should be given a chance to go as far as your God-given ability will take you" (as quoted in Hochschild and Scovronick 2003, 9).

Today in education, technology has become a critical part of that dream, offering the promise of preparing students for the challenges and opportunities of the twenty-first century. Middle-class parents assessing the quality of schools at every level often want to know, What is the student-to-computer ratio in the classrooms? Is there a separate computer lab? How is technology integrated throughout the curriculum? Is there a laptop program? A *New York Times* article about a visit to the Columbia University laboratory elementary school captures the draw of and early expectation for computers:

To a visitor, the school seemed a dream come true in many respects. Classes average about 18 students, and each class has two teachers. There were high-tech touches everywhere. Instead of chalkboards, there were big display screens tied to computers. Fourth-grade students had their own laptops, and teachers used their generous budgets to buy digital cameras. (Arenson 2004)

Today, a wired school and updated computer equipment are generally associated with academic advantage. This perception is frequently all the more embedded in otherwise-underresourced urban schools, where people breathe a sigh of relief if the school has been fortunate enough to acquire high-tech equipment and resources. In these schools, there is the hope—despite other socioeconomic disadvantages—that students are being given the tools necessary for success, fueling the belief that the presence of technology will help overcome social and institutional disparities. A *Los Angeles Times* article (Mehren 2002) about a new $37 million laptop program intended to ensure that all Maine seventh graders will have their own laptops cites educational administrators lauding the program for its effort to "level the academic playing field": "With the flip of a laptop 'on' switch, [the administrators] asserted, students who live in rusty trailers stood on a tech par with classmates whose seaside mansions boast broadband connections and troves of software."

Further hoping that technology will be the effective solution to increase learning and decrease the achievement gap, for decades those who make public policy have worked to get schools equipped with computers and connected to the Internet. Indeed, national data now show that the number and quality of computers in schools serving low-income students and students of color have steadily increased, and that there is now "virtually no difference in access between poor schools and their wealthier counterparts" (Fox 2005, 40). Yet our research reveals that irrespective of the kinds of technology available on campus, a key equity issue has been ignored: technology has not become the great equalizer, because schools are providing different learning opportunities, and these opportunities vary according to the racial and socioeconomic demographics of the students. More precisely, not just in our study but nationwide, schools serving higher numbers of white and wealthy students are more likely to offer a fuller array of college-bound instruction taught by experienced, qualified teachers, including in computer science, while schools serving the largest numbers of low-income students of color are more likely to offer lower-level courses, such as a technology curriculum limited to low-level computer literacy skills taught by teachers who, as we saw, often must "learn as they go" (Oakes et al. 2006). Belief systems within the schools then justify these disparities. And computer science education, it turns out, is a window through which we witness the serious contradictions of educational reform and the American dream.

In *Stuck in the Shallow End*, we wanted to understand the day-to-day school realities and the dynamics behind the statistics of underrepresentation in computer science. What we discovered was an interaction between institutional norms and belief systems impacting why so few African American and Latino/a high school students are learning computer science. What also became visible is how the computer science pipeline is an indicator of other critical educational disparities. Overall, for instance, less than one half (45 percent) of California's comprehensive high schools offer enough college preparatory classes to enable all students to take them. More than 25 percent of California high schools routinely assign inadequately trained teachers to college preparatory courses, and 33 percent assign inadequately trained teachers to college preparatory mathematics classes. California ranks last among the states in the provision of counselors; across the state, the average high school counselor has a caseload of 506 students—nearly double the national average. And schools with high concentrations of Latino/a and African American students have fewer of these essential college-preparation resources and opportunities than other schools (Oakes et al. 2006, iv). All of these factors together spell disaster for a system that claims to provide an equal playing field.

### Why We Object to the Notion of the Best and the Brightest

In 2006, we attended a conference in Washington, DC, sponsored by the National Center for Women and Information Technology (NCWIT).[1] The meeting brought together invited government representatives, computer science educators (from higher education and K–12), representatives from the computer industry who are concerned with the lack of diversity in their ranks, and representatives from national organizations who are committed to broadening the participation in computing. As part of the conference, a Washington "town meeting" on "IT Innovation and Diversity" was convened, and there a panel discussion focused on recent policy initiatives directed at increasing mathematics and science expertise in the United States. One of the panelists, a representative from the American Competitiveness Initiative, was asked about the lack of discussion concerning diversity in the initiative goals.[2] In her response, the initiative's representative admitted that there had been some "tension" around the drafting of the initiative because the drafters did not want to leave the impression that they wanted to widen the net so much as to let in anyone *less than* "the best and the brightest." The implication was clear: the best and the brightest was largely incongruous with balanced representation among racial groups. In response to this admission, an African American computer science professor, who is both a highly regarded computer scientist and a mentor to many students of color, jumped to his feet to respond. In remarks that were heartfelt and angry, he asserted, "All this talk about 'the best and the brightest' makes me sick." It was a righteous moment that woke everybody up.

The obvious question is, What's wrong with the best and the brightest? After all, the future of innovation depends on having original, creative thinking, and doesn't this typically come from the sharpest minds? Is it not an imperative? In fact, this descriptor (or any other company-specific nomenclature that means the same thing) is one of those assumptions and part of the way that Silicon Valley, and almost every academic department or employer, wants to see itself. And this professor was quick to acknowledge that this is the case, saying that he himself wants to find the best students for his own department. But he noted that over and over again, he has seen how the measuring stick most commonly used to determine who is the best and the brightest is faulty, based on biased, imperfect measures; in his view, tests like the SAT are self-fulfilling instruments created by the very "types" of people who will benefit from them. By following his own students' careers, he has witnessed how SAT test scores and other standardized testing, the normal standards of merit, do not accurately measure who will excel as a student or on the job.

Indeed, his observations have been confirmed by one of the most authoritative research projects to examine this issue. *The Shape of the River*, written by William Bowen and Derek Bok (1998), was the result of an unprecedented study of the academic and career histories of more than forty-five thousand students of all races who attended academically selective universities between 1970 and the early 1990s. Their study was an examination of how the normative way of evaluating admissions—prior grades and numerical test scores—"offer a tempting means of defining qualifications, since they are easily compiled and compared," yet their research found that these approaches are insufficient in what they tell us and in determining what students' future contributions will be. And so the best and the brightest, as measured in traditional terms, may not be either of these things.

Our research shows another dimension to why this phrase is so profoundly disturbing. The history of our country is one in which people of color (and in many cases, females) have historically been placed at the bottom of the intellectual hierarchy, far from the lofty reaches where the best and the brightest reside (Gould 1996). Further, as our educational system now assures, only those with preparatory privilege, including quality education and meaningful outside experiences with complex subject matter, will come close to meeting the profile expected of the best and the brightest. As we have seen in this research project, students of color in low-resourced high schools who are most often denied access to learning opportunities, mentors, or sufficient preparation that are so sorely needed, are disadvantaged from the starting gate (Lee and Burkam 2002).[3] This inequality then follows students throughout their entire education as our system gives less to the students most in need. And so the best and the brightest really comes to mean "the blessed and the privileged."

Of course, there are the exceptions—individuals who come from schools such as the ones we have studied and who have defied the odds. There are clearly individuals who find ways to make their dreams come true. But even recognizing the existence and importance of individual agency, determination, and courage, we cannot account for the vast amount of talent that remains lost or hidden from view. And this is why these individuals still remain as the so-called exceptions. Basic facilitators like access to resources, mentors, preparation, and learning opportunities are too often absent in schools such as the ones we have studied. Furthermore, even when the exceptions make it through the barriers, they have had to face and overcome years and years of continuous doubt (from themselves and others) about whether they really are the best and the brightest, simply because of their race or gender.

So phrases and words such as "the best and the brightest" and "the exceptions" are freighted with the history of racism and inequality. And of course, as always with language, it matters who says it and in what context. While some may decide to reappropriate the language, and use "the best and the brightest" to describe underrepresented students as a way of acknowledging all of the unrecognized, untapped, and lost talent (and we are tempted to do this as well), at this point we believe that the phrase is mostly used mindlessly, with no awareness of the deep structural inequities that keep so many students in low-resourced schools "stuck in the shallow end," ultimately written off, and unable to realize their full potential. They have been robbed. And they are largely unseen.

To us, it appeared that the American Competitiveness Initiative speaker was completely oblivious to how she had revealed widely held and deep-seated assumptions about race, equity, and excellence. Yet for us, she had blown the issue wide open. A document from Project Science, Engineering, Equity, and Diversity, which is affiliated with the Civil Rights Project, most poignantly captures how science, technology, engineering, and mathematics fields "are among the most heavily guarded, prestigious arenas, and reserved for 'the best and the brightest'": "Due to the prevalent racist assumptions that racial equity and excellence are incompatible goals, these fields are still the most segregated and conservative" (Ong and Park 2006).[4] Our own research sadly supports this assertion completely, revealing the structural factors that maintain the inequitable and unjust status quo.

## A Tale of Three Schools

As we crisscrossed the larger metropolitan area of Los Angeles, investigating one specific point in the educational landscape—who is (or is not) learning computer science at the high school level—a whole world of inequality came on us. We witnessed the structural constraints of a large, overcrowded school; we saw higher-level, more rigorous classes offered in a school with high numbers of white students, but not in schools with higher concentrations of students of color; we saw the testing frenzy, fueled by reform initiatives created under the guise of helping students, yet that actually distract from the business of educating them; and we heard all sorts of rationales for the inequalities we were witnessing, and saw the extent to which these rationales become normalized in the minds of both teachers and students.

While there are particulars associated with computer science (its status as an elective, not a core requirement, for example) that made the investigation at times challenging, even messy, we ultimately identified a full array of factors that were impacting students' chances to go to college, their entire futures, whether they would ever be considered as among the best and the brightest—for after all, that is how computer scientists are often identified.[5] What we discovered is powerfully rendered by Simmons College professor Theresa Perry in her afterword to *Can We Talk about Race?* Here, Perry addresses the "role that race has and continues to play in determining who has access to what kind of education." She describes a documentary film that compares the differences between an inner-city school and one in an overwhelmingly white suburb:

After you have watched the presentation, it is hard to get out of your mind the plaintive voice of a Black male from the city school as he talks about wanting to enroll in an honors algebra class and twice being closed out because of limited space. His comment is positioned alongside that of a suburban White student who, in her privileged environment, rattles off quickly—as if to suggest that so much is available that she might miss something if she goes slowly—the range and diversity of course offerings, in addition to numerous honors and AP classes in virtually all content areas. (Perry 2007, 128)

These words capture the haunting feeling we had after visiting East River, Westward, and then Canyon, the three schools of our study. Likewise, we concur with Perry's observation that "an ideological discourse holds sway in the public domain that blames these students, their peer groups, their parents, and their communities for their underperformance in school" (129–130).

From our travels, we also heard this ideological discourse, and we saw its role in masking, justifying, and rationalizing disparities in learning opportunities that fall along socioeconomic and racial lines. We saw how belief systems that link different racial groups to different capacities and propensities are often so deeply entrenched that sometimes we no longer even see them. And we saw how these belief systems interact with structural inequities to make a powerful mechanism that ends up preselecting only a narrow band of students to receive the necessary preparation for the twenty-first-century economic world.

### Returning to Our Unlikely Metaphor

We opened our book drawing parallels between the underrepresentation of African Americans and Latinos in computer science, and the history of segregation in swimming. We went this unusual route because we could not walk another path after learning what we did about the history of swimming: the parallels were too great, the symbolic danger of exclusion from computer science was too strong a match for the history of segregation in swimming. The history of swimming foreshadows an interaction of factors (structural norms and belief systems) that are related to the underrepresentation in computer science, but are more easily illuminated when considering an activity less esoteric than computer science.

This year at the 2008 Beijing Summer Olympics, it is possible that we may see only one or possibly two U.S. swim team members who are swimmers of color. These swimmers are still among the exceptions.[6] In years past, the absence of swimmers of color has just been taken for granted, barely questioned by the general public. Now, because of the ongoing USA Swimming diversity campaign and the Nike endorsement of African American swimmer Cullen Jones, there is likely to be media attention on these swimmers in the months leading up to the Olympic games.[7] We can only hope that more of the story behind the statistics of swimming as a supposedly white sport will be revealed, only now on a more public scale and perhaps with greater effect.

As athletes and fans watch these swimmers dive into the waters of the Beijing Olympic pool, we hope that people will become more aware of the violent history that has preceded these dives, and how this history is still to this day having tragic consequences. We hope that conversations about the racial makeup of the sport will be sparked, challenging what has been expected and seen as normal. In the same way, we hope that educators who are committed to equity will consider our metaphor, not as a random choice or simply a literary device, but as a useful entry point for thinking about the spaces and subjects in schools that either don't exist or are still segregated, and then talk with others about why this is so. And ultimately we hope these conversations will help open access to the deeper waters of education for all students.

# Afterword

Richard Tapia

I am a Chicano (Latino, if you wish) and a mathematician, a product of the Los Angeles Unified School District. Fifty years ago, I was in eleventh grade at Narbonne High School in Lomita, California, widely perceived at the time as one of LAUSD's lowest performing high schools. The principal had announced there would be a mathematics test given to the entire school and the student with the highest score would be given a medal at a school-wide assembly. I was not motivated strongly by school, more into cars than books, but I knew I was good in math. I wanted to do well on that test, win the medal, and receive the acknowledgement I knew I deserved but had never received.

I *did* earn the highest score on the test, but rather than being awarded my medal in front of my peers as promised, the principal did not schedule the assembly and instead gave me the prize in his office. I was hugely disappointed and angry at what felt like a judgment that I was unfit to be honored by the school. So angry, in fact, that today, fifty years later, it still bothers me. This was certainly not the first time I had an experience like this, nor would it be the last. I always felt that I was smart and from first grade to twelfth grade was among the best in the school in math. But, with the exception of my fifth grade teacher, Mrs. Bentwood, none of my teachers or counselors acknowledged me, complimented me, or encouraged me. No teacher or counselor said that I was smart or told me that I should (or could) go to college.

In contrast, I came from a home where I was taught—and where I witnessed—confidence and determination. My father and mother, both of whom came to Los Angeles from Mexico with the odds stacked against them, were the hardest working people I have ever met. My father taught the value of inclusion—he loved everyone and they loved him. My mother taught me that pride in being Mexican, hard work, and education can take you any place you want to go. She was aware that her message was in contrast to more widely held beliefs in our community and spent a good amount of time dealing with this conflict, helping us to maintain our pride and belief that we could: *si se puede*.

But, as *Stuck in the Shallow End: Education, Race, and Computing* demonstrates, the forces within a school are powerful, and once I graduated from Narbonne, I did not use or build on my mathematical talents; instead, I went to work in a factory making mufflers. I packed fiberglass in the hot sun next to a fellow employee named Jim, who was white, in his forties, and married with four kids. Every day he said, "Richard, you are smart. Don't make the same mistake that I made. Go to college." Thanks to his encouragement, two months later I enrolled in Harbor Junior College in Wilmington, California, where I excelled, especially in math and chemistry. Two of my professors, Stuart Friedman and David Frisch, told me in very strong terms that I was going to UCLA, and I agreed.

I was not a star as an undergraduate at UCLA, but my "B's" were good, and I learned a lot of math. During my senior year, two of my friends told me that they were going to continue their study of mathematics in graduate school. Relying on a logic I had developed in the absence of meaningful feedback from others, I told myself that I was better than they were, so I should go to graduate school, too. Just as in high school (and just like the students in *Stuck in the Shallow End*), I found my way to the next level of education much by chance, with little help from those who should have been looking out for me.

Graduate school was a natural fit for me, and I did well. As I neared completion of my PhD at UCLA, David Sanchez, the only Mexican American Professor in the Mathematics Department, asked me about my plans. I was unsure, but he believed in me; following that conversation, he worked with the chair of the Mathematics Department to secure me a postdoctoral offer from the University of Wisconsin–Madison, which turned out to be the best place in the world for me. There, I worked with several of the world's finest mathematicians and established a strong network that has lasted me a lifetime. More than thirty years ago I transitioned from Wisconsin to Rice University in Houston, Texas, where I have built my career.

When I agreed to read *Stuck in the Shallow End*, I thought I would experience a somewhat pleasant journey down memory lane. After all, I was one of the students you just read about; I have been there—or so I thought. As I began to read, the critically important message of the book immediately hit me, and my understanding quickly turned to anger and frustration: costly and highly touted technology and computer education programs, billed as closing the minority-majority education gap, are not only failing, they are actually widening the gap in a dangerous manner.

Sadly, the misuse of technology is not new. Years back, I shocked many in the K–12 mathematics teaching community by saying that calculators would be widely misused and, in most cases, preclude higher-level thinking and understanding. Indeed, I have seen young clerks at stores use calculators to calculate eight times ten. One told me that he could not complete my sale because his calculator was not working, and I had purchased six items. (I just added the prices for him.) I often ask K–12 math teachers, how do you find the square root of a number? They have no idea and believe that there is no value in knowing because, after all, the calculator will do it for you. In a high school math book I actually read the statement: "The correlation coefficient is what you get when you push the correlation coefficient button on your calculator." What a travesty. The misuse of technology precludes good mathematics. And as we have learned from the case studies in this book, this misuse is derived from and leads to significant inequities.

As a professor at Rice University's Department of Computational and Applied Mathematics, I have taught undergraduate and graduate students in the computing sciences for more than three decades. I know firsthand that minority representation is not increasing in these fields—it is actually decreasing at the graduate level. The simple and convenient scapegoat would be the failing K–12 schools or, more broadly, society in general, but to leave it at that does not acknowledge the particulars of what is happening in K–12 computer science—to leave it at that is not acceptable. Every educator and educational policy maker should read *Stuck in the Shallow End*, and in doing so they will see how naive we are as a nation in thinking that we are on the right path.

Over the years, I have developed an extreme dislike for the expression "the best and the brightest," so the authors' discussion of it in the concluding chapter particularly resonated with me. I have seen extremely talented and creative underrepresented minority undergraduate students aggressively excluded from this distinction. While serving on a National Science review panel years back, I learned that to be included in this category you had to have been doing science by the age of ten. Of course, because of lack of opportunities, few underrepresented minorities qualified.

In high school I was one of the "best and the brightest," but my teachers, counselors, and administrators never recognized it. I did not fit their idea of the model student, and being of Mexican descent certainly did not help. Many now consider me an "exception," a university mathematics professor who is Chicano. But I maintain that I am not that unusual, and there are many underrepresented minorities out there with similar or more creativity who could follow the same path if given the opportunities. If we identify and nurture all students who show innovation and creativity—even though, like me, they may not fall under traditional notions of the "best and the brightest"—we can produce "exceptions" to the point that minority scholars and scientists are simply the norm.

*Stuck in the Shallow End* is a warning to all of us. It is well timed, coming on the heels of the recent, highly visible report, *Rising above the Gathering Storm: Energizing and Employing America for a Brighter Economic Future* (or, *RAGS*), mandated by Congress and facilitated and published by the National Academies (2007). Like *Stuck in the Shallow End*, the *RAGS* report is also a warning; it warns the nation that we are in danger of losing our world leadership in science and technology innovation and at risk of not being able to fill our need for high-end technical jobs. Many, including this writer, have stated that the nation's greatest hope of avoiding these dangers is to turn to our underrepresented groups, namely, women and underrepresented minorities. Yet, *Stuck in the Shallow End* shines a glaring light on the fact that we are far from doing so. Instead, as a nation, we are spending huge amounts of money to move in directions away from—rather than toward—those solutions that *RAGS* has identified.

A clear message of this book is that better computer science, indeed science, will not come from being stuck in the shallow end, no matter how good the technology is at that end of the pool, because the tools are not being used properly. Minority students in high school are in danger of being made technologically rich but cognitively poor. In the shallow end they are not encouraged to be innovative or to pursue paths leading to high-end technology jobs. Yet this is what the nation so desperately needs. Better technology comes from better science and better science comes from the proper use of better technology. It is a cycle, to be sure, but it need not be a vicious one. Students simply need clearer pathways into it and support once they arrive.

The authors' use of the historical color line in swimming as an analogy refreshes our memories and keeps us aware of the incredible obstacles that many of us have had to face. The familiarity that this imagery offers makes it much more difficult to deny our circumstance or to presume we have done enough. *Stuck in the Shallow End* is a powerful warning. America, take heed.

# Appendix A
# Methodology: Process and Reflections

In most investigations like ours, a tension exists between the original suppositions that shape the research design and the need to have a clear mind, listening to what emerges from and is grounded in the data.[1] The plan is essential for ensuring consistency and focus in data collection, and an open mind is vital to ensuring that the project remains connected to the realities of those being studied. Given that, in this appendix we review the strategies we used to collect and analyze our data, but we also discuss the challenges we encountered and the lessons we learned about doing this type of research. Rather than a just a straightforward account of the details of data collection and analysis, we offer more of a behind-the-scenes account that problematizes what is often presented as a seamless research process (Weis and Fine 2000, 2).[2] We reflect on the issues that caused us difficulty, how we resolved them (or did not resolve them), and what we see as important aspects of future studies. We write this to be helpful to other researchers who are engaged in qualitative research in high schools, specifically those focused on issues of race, class, and gender.

## Our Framework and Research Questions

Our framework for investigating the complex factors impacting students' decisions about whether or not to learn computer science is based on a model formulated by Jeannie Oakes (1989) in her article "Tracking in Mathematics and Science Education: A Structural Contribution to Unequal Schooling." Applying this model to the computer science pipeline, we were guided by the theoretical proposition that there is an "intricate interplay" between two sets of factors:

• *The high school educational environment*    A school's structures of opportunity for learning computer science, such as computer science course offerings, tracking norms, prerequisites, resources, teacher availability, and training
• *Psychological and cultural factors*    Issues of students' motivations to learn computer science, their sense of the importance or unimportance of computing, access and home computing environments, cultural assumptions of who will and will not succeed in computer science, race and gender stereotypes, and peer and friendship patterns and dynamics

Our research methods were directed at examining the dynamic that exists between these microlevel and macrolevel issues. Two related grants, "Out of the Loop" and "Constructing the Pipeline," allowed us to focus on the perspectives and experiences of students and educators in the schools.[3] "Out of the Loop" concentrated on students' perspectives, and for this portion of the project we were guided by two related research questions:

• What are the institutional and structural aspects of high school computer science education that narrow the information technology pipeline for different groups of underrepresented minority and women students?
• What are the psychosocial and cultural factors linked to studying computer science that could be affecting college-bound underrepresented minority students' interest in, motivation, and decisions to pursue information technology?

"Constructing the Pipeline" allowed us to examine educators' roles in shaping the pipeline. For this aspect of the research we were guided by the following questions:

• How do educators at the high school level frame their understanding of the purposes of computer science education?
• How do they judge the capacity and needs of their student body as well as individual students to learn computer science?
• How does educators' sense making of these issues translate into the structures and institutional norms of computer science learning at the high school level?
• How do these norms and structures widen or narrow the computer science pipeline for underrepresented minority and female high school students?

We sought answers to these two sets of questions at three public high schools scattered across urban Los Angeles.

## Site Selection

We chose to do our research at East River, Westward, and Canyon because these schools were similar in their connection to the Digital High School program, and in their large percentage of students of color. But the specifics of their student demographics varied, and this afforded an important contrast that allowed us to shed additional light on our research issues. As we described in earlier chapters, East River has a largely Latino/a population, Westward is primarily African American, and Canyon is the most diverse of the three campuses, with roughly half of the students (48 percent) identifying as African American or Latino/a. Table A.1 summarizes student racial demographics at the three schools as well as additional measures that speak to the socioeconomic and cultural characteristics of the students on each of the three campuses.

We have found that computer science learning opportunities are often indicative of the disparities in more general learning opportunities, and these disparities frequently fall along race and socioeconomic lines.

Table A.1
Student characteristics by school site (2003–4 academic year)

|  | East River | Westward | Canyon |
|---|---|---|---|
| Total student enrollment | 4,855 | 2,545 | 2,634 |
| *Race/Ethnicity of Students* | | | |
| African American | 0% | 64% | 23% |
| Latino/a | 98% | 26% | 25% |
| Filipino | 0% | 0% | 1% |
| Asian | 0% | 2% | 8% |
| White | 1% | 7% | 42% |
| American Indian | 0% | 0% | 0% |
| *Additional student characteristics* | | | |
| Students who are English-language learners | 35% | 10% | 9% |
| Students receiving free or reduced-cost lunches | 93% | 31% | 27% |
| Students with at least one parent who is a high school graduate | 64% | 88% | 91% |
| Students with at least one parent who is a college graduate | 9% | 46% | 61% |

*Source*: California Department of Education, California Basic Educational Data System, School Information Form

**Table A.2**
Academic indicators by school site (2003–4 academic year)

| | East River | Westward | Canyon |
|---|---|---|---|
| Academic Performance Index (API; growth)[*] | 557 | 608 | 756 |
| API state-comparison decile[**] | 2 | 3 | 10 |
| Number of AP courses offered | 8 | 10 | 17 |
| Percentage of students enrolled in advanced mathematics | 5.6% | 6.3% | 14.3% |
| Graduation rate[***] | 39.3% | 47.0% | 62.6% |
| Percentage of students who have completed college requirements on graduation[***] | 12.9% | 16.1% | 36.7% |

[*]API scores range from two hundred to one thousand, and are based on results from statewide tests; schools with API scores lower than eight hundred must meet annual target scores until they reach eight hundred
[**] In the API base reports, schools are ranked in ten categories of equal size, called deciles, from one (lowest) to ten (highest); a school's statewide rank compares that school to other schools of the same type (in this case, high schools) in the entire state
[***]Based on ninth-grade cohort data
*Source*: California Department of Education, California Basic Educational Data System, School Information Form

If we widen the lens and look beyond computer science to other indicators, such as enrollment in mathematics and AP classes and whether or not students graduate having met the requirements for college admission, these disparities become even clearer. This is yet another reminder that computer science education cannot be studied outside a larger context of the entire educational system. These academic indicators are summarized in table A.2.

## Data Collection

Our research strategies were very much influenced by qualitative and ethnographic traditions. We believed in the importance of becoming familiar with the day-to-day details and dynamics of computer science learning in the schools in order to make apparent what is normally obscured by more distant and predominantly statistical accounts. In addition, we strove to become familiar with the larger context of the computer science pipeline itself—the state of the educational environments (the cultures, structures, norms, standards, and beliefs) of each school. We also believed that key to understanding students' decisions and pathways in and out of the computer science pipeline was knowledge of the perspectives of the students and educators themselves within the context of this environment (Merriam 1998).

Our data collection methods consisted of one-on-one interviews and focus group discussions, both of which were guided by interview protocols based on our overarching research questions. To supplement these data sources, we conducted regular informal observations of classrooms, labs, and after-school activities during our frequent visits to the schools. The information we gleaned from these observations enabled us to provide the necessary context for analyzing our interviews and identify areas deserving of further attention.

Before we began collecting data, we met with the LAUSD director of science. He became an advocate for our research, and facilitated our access and data gathering in the district schools. We also met with the principal in each school to explain the issues behind our study and chosen methodology, and ask for any thoughts they had about our research. The principals then facilitated our access to the teachers and students.

## "Out of the Loop" Student Interviews

We struggled long and hard to determine the criteria and selection process for students to interview, in particular because we were concerned about consistency across all three schools in spite of the inevitable curricular differences. Ultimately, because we were interested in students pursuing computer science and students who were qualified to pursue it yet were not doing so, we chose to interview ninth- to eleventh-grade college-bound students who were currently enrolled in either the most advanced computer science course offered in the school or upper-level math classes. We surmised that interviewing from the most advanced computer science classes would give us a collective portrait of some of the most techie students in the school, while interviewing students from upper-level mathematics classes included those with the necessary prerequisites and preparation for more advanced computer science classes, whether they had enrolled or not.

Despite our best intentions to create some sort of consistency across the three schools, the course offerings changed significantly in two of the schools during the first year of our research, so what qualified as "the most advanced computer science course" turned out to be a moving target. For instance, when we began the research in 2001, a programming class was offered in two of the schools (East River and Canyon) and AP computer science was offered in two (Westward and Canyon) as well. But within the first two years of data collection, the programming class was canceled at East River and the AP computer science class was canceled at Westward, leaving Internet publishing as the only class beyond the introductory level at the two schools with the highest concentrations of students of color. This reduction in course offerings became a significant finding about the disparities in learning opportunities within and between schools, but these changes also forced us to choose additional classes in each school from which to draw students. Because we ended up interviewing from less advanced classes, the range of students (academically speaking) within and between schools was wider than we had originally intended.

To solicit student participation, we gave a recruiting speech in each class, describing the purpose of the research and asking for volunteer participants. Occasionally, the teacher would give us a recommendation of a student he or she believed would be a particularly informative participant. Before students could be interviewed they had to have permission slips signed by their parents. This resulted in several returns to the school before the interviews could be conducted.

Scheduling and conducting interviews proved to be challenging at the high school level. In overcrowded schools like those we were visiting, there are frequently no available rooms, so it was not uncommon for us to conduct our interviews outside on the ground or in the back of a noisy classroom. Although we would have loved to spend hours with each student, often we were only given short blocks of time (such as twenty-five minutes) for each interview. This forced us to prioritize our interview questions, skipping some and adding others, in order to learn the most important information about the student.

To supplement our interview data we also conducted several focus groups with college-bound students. We discussed this idea with several of the teachers at Canyon who were specifically in charge of widening the academic pathways of students of color at the school, through programs like Mathematics, Engineering, Science, Achievement (MESA) and Advancement Via Individual Determination (AVID).[4] As persons of color themselves, these teachers agreed that the level of trust they had built with their students was a key ingredient to having more open discussions.

Table A.3
Demographic breakdown of student participants by school site

| | Number of students | | | |
|---|---|---|---|---|
| | East River | Westward | Canyon | Total |
| *Race (as identified by student)* | | | | |
| Latino/a | 60 | 8 | 16 | 84 |
| African American | 0 | 29 | 11 | 40 |
| White/other | 0 | 9* | 36** | 45 |
| Asian/other | 0 | 4 | 12 | 16 |
| *Gender* | | | | |
| Male | 29 | 28 | 39 | 96 |
| Female | 31 | 22 | 36 | 89 |
| Total | 60 | 50 | 75 | 185 |

* Westward white/other includes two Israelis, one Persian, and one Egyptian
** Canyon white/other includes seven Russians and seven Persians

They agreed to lead student discussions with students of color that we could sit in on and observe. And so in April 2003, four student discussions were held on our research topic—two with students involved in MESA and two with students involved in AVID. The MESA students were predominantly Latino/a and the AVID students were predominantly African American, although each group had several students of other races.

Between our interviews and focus groups, we spoke with a total of 185 students. Table A.3 shows the demographic breakdown of our student participants.

Table A.4 lists by school the courses and activities from which we recruited students, and the numbers of students from each who were interviewed or participated in the focus groups.

## The Student Interview Guide and Process

Initially, we determined the themes we wanted to learn about and then created the interview guides. These guides were designed to ensure that the questions were open-ended enough so that the participants could "tell their own story" and not be constrained by our prior assumptions, while being focused enough to capture what we hypothesized to be the critical areas for investigation. Our questions were structured to elicit students' thoughts about their knowledge of, experiences with, and motivations to

**Table A.4**
Courses and activities from which student sample was drawn by school site (interviews and focus groups)

|  | Number of students | | | |
|---|---|---|---|---|
|  | East River | Westward | Canyon | Total |
| *Computer courses* | | | | |
| Programming | 6 | n/a | 22 | 28 |
| Internet publishing | 5 | 23 | n/a | 28 |
| Video production | 22 | n/a | n/a | 22 |
| AP computer science | n/a | n/a | 19 | 19 |
| Data processing | n/a | n/a | 24 | 24 |
| *Total* | *33* | *23* | *65* | *121* |
| *Mathematics courses* | | | | |
| Intermediate algebra/precalculus | 26 | 0 | 0 | 26 |
| Math analysis | 0 | 9 | 0 | 9 |
| AP calculus | 0 | 8 | 0 | 8 |
| *Total* | *26* | *17* | *0* | *43* |
| *Other courses* | | | | |
| Social studies | 0 | 0 | 2 | 2 |
| *Total* | *0* | *0* | *2* | *2* |
| *Other activities* | | | | |
| After-school robotics club | 1 | n/a | n/a | 1 |
| Leadership | n/a | 8 | n/a | 8 |
| Computer science service bureau | n/a | 2 | n/a | 2 |
| AVID | n/a | n/a | 8 | 8 |
| *Total* | *1* | *10* | *8* | *19* |
| **Total** | **60** | **50** | **75** | **185** |

learn computer science. We also asked more generally about their academic backgrounds and school experiences. The full interview protocol was based on seven broad themes:

1. Family and computing background
2. Schooling opportunities and experiences
3. Interests in computing: Where do they come from? How do they stay alive?
4. Identity: Do students see themselves belonging in this field? How? Why? Why not? Friendship groups and social networks?
5. Understanding of "What is computer science?" and students' images of computer scientists

6. Do students see themselves belonging in computer science? How? Why? Why not?

7. Students' views on diversity in computer science, and why the field is predominantly white, Asian, and male

As often happens in qualitative research, our student interview guide changed multiple times over the three years in response to changes within the schools and to what we were learning. At the outset, for example, we were interested in hearing about students' technology expertise, and this was the focus of early interview protocols. Yet it was not long before there was significant redundancy in what we were hearing from students about this issue, and we also felt that our interview protocol was too centered on computers. We were not learning enough about the subjects and topics that students found more (or less) interesting than computer science, and what their more general attitudes toward school were. This was an important transition, because without a fuller portrait of each student, we felt we could not properly evaluate how they sized up the significance of learning computer science for their own life plans and interests. Other changes in the protocol were similarly implemented as our understanding about how school norms were impacting students' "decisions" about studying and learning computer science. So while our questions were always connected to the themes listed above, our interview guide did change over the three-year research span.

## "Constructing the Pipeline" Educator Interviews

In spite of their keen insights about the sorting process in schools, there are certain influences that students cannot report on because they take place outside of their view or simply without their knowledge. So while we knew that students are irreplaceable informants about proximal gatekeepers because they can immediately see, experience, and identify the influences that encourage or discourage them from further engagement with computer science opportunities, we also knew there was more to the story. For example, we saw how students were often unaware of the larger patterns and institutional structures within their schools that were instrumental in their access to and experiences within the computer science pipeline. We therefore found it necessary to conduct a set of in-depth interviews with adult policy setters, which when combined with the student interviews, would allow us to understand more fully the institutional structures and norms that shape the computer science pipeline for underrepresented students. "Constructing the Pipeline" interviews included the principals, computer science teachers, technology coordinators, counselors, magnet coordinators, mathematics teachers, and teachers in other classes that may have involved technology in the three schools. In addition, we interviewed key district administrators involved in the writing and implementing of state and district technology plans.

The educators we interviewed from our case study schools held the following positions and/or taught the following classes:

• *Westward*   Principal, vice principal, college counselor, past instructor of programming and AP computer science, Internet publishing teacher, technology coordinator, applications teacher, mathematics teacher, magnet coordinator, art teacher, social studies teacher, and leadership team
• *East River*   Principal, vice principal, college counselor, introduction to computing teacher, Internet publishing teacher, programming teacher, mathematics teacher, video production teacher, and technology coordinator
• *Canyon*   Principal, vice principal, college counselor, AP computer science teacher, programming teacher, mathematics teacher, social studies teacher, AVID coordinator, MESA coordinator, and Media Academy coordinator

In all, we interviewed thirty educators from our three schools (sometimes multiple times) as well as twelve computer science teachers who came from other schools, but had participated in our summer institute. We also had numerous conversations with the LAUSD director of science and the instructional technology facilitator who was the liaison to our project.

The themes we discussed with the educators included: teachers' personal teaching histories; the computer science curriculum in their school; their views on enrollment demographics in their classes; their views on what type of students do well in computer science; their views on why so many students are underrepresented in computer science and how to broaden the pipeline; and their descriptions of how they teach computer science and what makes it meaningful for their students. As with the student interview protocol, our set of questions for educators evolved over time, but always connected back to our core study issues.

## Data Analysis

All of our interviews and focus groups were audiotaped. After each interview, the interviewer wrote a narrative summary to capture the important points of the conversation and document developing themes. During weekly meetings we would continuously compare analyses for reliability, update interview questions and themes to code for, and chart new relationships between our findings. As new themes emerged, these ideas were probed in subsequent interviews. Each interview was transcribed, and then analyzed according to our growing list of themes and categories. We employed the computer qualitative analysis software package ATLAS.ti., which allowed us to generate reports on themes across interviews and subsets of students.

In the end, an extensive list of codes was used in the analysis of student interviews, as summarized in table A.5 below. A similarly comprehensive list of codes was employed for our educator interviews, as summarized below in table A.6. It should be noted that while we have grouped our codes here in order to more clearly present them, they were not bracketed this way during the coding process. As we analyzed the data, the individual codes were kept discrete, allowing us to combine and condense as necessary or appropriate once all the interviews had been analyzed.

With all of these categories coded, we then looked for *patterns* across the data. Where was the coherence across the individual interviews? What were the themes that tied the stories together (Luttrell 1997)? These themes then became our findings.

As individuals and a team, we remained self-reflective as we conducted this research project. Throughout the data collection and analysis as well as in the writing process, we have asked ourselves—as others have asked us—what we would do differently next time. Our suggestions for ourselves and others who may undertake similar projects in the future touch on issues of effective data collection methods along with interviewer selection and assignment; we have gained insight into better ways to access and understand overcrowded schools; and we have learned valuable lessons about making sense of the delicate and complicated issues of race and gender inequity. These reflections are summarized in the remainder of this appendix.

## Asking about and Listening for Race

At the core of our research is a sensitive and difficult topic: race. It is not surprising, then, that one of our biggest challenges turned out to be coming up with the right ways to ask about the topic. The issues of inequality that we were exploring are not always easy to discuss, and this is

**Table A.5**
Coding categories: Student interviews

| Grouping | Specific coding category |
| --- | --- |
| Home context | • Parents' jobs, educational backgrounds, and ethnic backgrounds<br>• Resource issues<br>• Siblings<br>• Home community<br>• Parents knowledge of computing<br>• Home computer access, use, and equipment |
| General interests | • Hobbies, passions, interests, and friendship groups<br>• Games they play? Games they like/dislike? |
| School context (descriptive) | • Description of their current schools<br>• Statements that address school technology access<br>• School use of computers outside of computer science or Internet publishing<br>• Are computer science classes electives or requirements? |
| Academic history and academic identity | • Prior schools, and reasons for attending each school<br>• Comments about themselves as a student<br>• Classes taken<br>• Favorite and weakest subjects<br>• Accomplishments in, status with, and relationship to math |
| Interest in technology | • What they want to learn in computing<br>• Statements that describe play with computing<br>• Decision-making process about taking computer science classes |
| Technology experience | • Personal networks related to computers<br>• Computing activities and skills<br>• How they learned computing, who taught them, and entry point<br>• Computing confidence<br>• What got them (or keeps them) hooked on computing |
| Plans for the future | • Plans for after high school? College?<br>• Thoughts about careers<br>• Relevance of computers to their future plans |
| Thoughts about computer science as a field | • Definition of programming<br>• Definition of computer science<br>• Reasons for the demographics (race and gender) in computer science<br>• Descriptions of students who are savvy with computers |

**Table A.5**
(continued)

| Grouping | Specific coding category |
|---|---|
| | • How they imagine computer scientists<br>• Statements about stereotypes<br>• Statements related to gender and computers<br>• Statements related to race and computers<br>• Can they picture themselves in the computer science world?<br>• Costs of computing materials (e.g., textbooks and equipment) |
| Perceptions of teachers | • Perceptions of and relationships with teachers<br>• Teachers' abilities in computer science |

especially true in the context of a research project. In our case, there were often significant differences between the interviewers and the students in terms of age, gender, and/or race, and we knew going in that these differences were likely to have an impact on the interview dynamic. Did the fact that we were older, or of different races, affect how they answered our questions? Were students comfortable enough, in the time we had with them, to move beyond the "color blindness" they may have been taught through various forms of multiculturalism, so prevalent in schools today? We were aware throughout that because of these and other related factors, students might not be able (or inclined) to reveal their true feelings, and they might respond by telling us what they thought we wanted to hear. Also, as mentioned earlier, we frequently had less time than we would have liked to complete our interviews, which meant less time to build trust and comfort—two important elements in ensuring data reliability, especially around sensitive topics.

For the duration of the project, we discussed how race and racial issues are often disguised or not articulated as race at all. We would sometimes hear from some students, for instance, that "everyone gets along" and that race is just not an issue at their schools; yet these same students could all point out where each race of students congregated, and it was clear that for the most part they congregated along racial lines.[5] In a sense, "getting along" seemed to be a euphemism about coexisting within a mixed-race school. In a similar vein, most students told us they believed that the computer industry was diverse in terms of race and gender. Yet

**Table A.6**
Coding categories: Educator interviews

| Grouping | Specific coding category |
|---|---|
| Background/ personal history | • Why became a teacher?<br>• Years in classroom, and what schools/courses<br>• Perceptions of school's reputation<br>• Computing background<br>• Professional development |
| Computing in the school | • Courses offered at the school<br>• Distinctions between different computer science courses<br>• Desired computer science course offerings<br>• How computer science fits into other school priorities<br>• Integration of computing in broader curriculum<br>• Perceived importance of computer science for students<br>• Other skills gained from programming |
| Enrollment in computer science classes | • Students' reasons for enrolling in computer science<br>• Students' preexisting skills with computer science<br>• Breakdown of skills by gender and race<br>• Required skills for success in computer science<br>• What students are taught in computer science<br>• Suggested prerequisites for computer science<br>• Computer science courses that should be requirements?<br>• Electives?<br>• Computer science and University of California requirements |
| Student enrollment by race and gender | • Class enrollment by race and gender<br>• Comparison of class enrollment to overall school population<br>• Perceptions of reasons for imbalance<br>• Enrolled students' future plans<br>• Perceptions of why some students do not take computing classes |
| What makes a good computer science student? | • Qualities of a "good" computer science student<br>• Description of a computer wiz (gender and race) |
| Course content/ curriculum | • Most successful assignments<br>• Least successful assignments<br>• Hooks to student engagement<br>• Greatest challenges and obstacles<br>• Missed opportunities in schools for engaging student interest |

**Table A.6**
(continued)

| Grouping | Specific coding category |
|---|---|
| Engaging different groups of students in computing | • Difficulties in recruiting/engaging students in computer science<br>• Perceived differences in engagement between different groups of students<br>• Reasons for gender and race imbalance in computer science as a whole<br>• Ideas for increasing interest among and success of underrepresented students |

when asked what their image of a computer scientist was, they almost all said white or Asian male, sometimes drawing on troubling racial stereotypes. By the same token, most students said that their computer classes were diverse, but when they were asked how many African Americans, Latinos/as, or females were in their classes, they had a difficult time answering us. Often, it seemed, these were genuine moments of race realization for them.

During our data analysis, the issues around race continued to challenge us. In an internal team memo titled "Appearing and Disappearing: Reading for Race in Interviews" we articulated the challenge this way:

How and where do we analyze for race in our interviews? What are the questions and responses that most capture issues of race? In fact, we have found that race is not discrete and can be found interwoven throughout the interviews. Furthermore, race often disappears when we ask about it and appears when we don't ask about it. Students are often not only answering as racial beings but they are also speaking from other parts of their identities, such as athlete, computer techie, or AP-achieving culture. People are not just embodiments of race, class, and gender. There is a danger of conflating culture with race and ethnicity alone, when there is the athlete culture, the nerd culture, the Internet publishing culture. The challenge is how to code and interpret these quotes and these identities.

Given these contradictions and complexities, and given that issues in education are "deeply marbled by class, race, and gender" (Weis and Fine 2000, 2), the question for us then became, As we code our data, what is associated with race and what is not? And while we did not arrive at a final answer to this question—the conversation is ongoing—simply asking it forced us to continuously monitor how we listened to the data. Ultimately, we were able to address these questions by constantly challenging each other and by drawing on our detailed observations of school dynamics, which were essential as we struggled to make sense of what we were hearing from students. These observations allowed us to place our interview and focus group data in their proper context, and thus be more certain of the reliability of our findings. In the end, we believe we have analyzed our data with an awareness of and sensitivity to these frequently unspoken realities of race (Luttrell 1997; Weis and Fine 2000).

## Additional Lessons for Future Research

We learned so much from the several years that we spent at East River, Westward, and Canyon. We are hopeful that our findings will contribute to the ongoing conversation about how to make our schools more equitable, just spaces. At the same time, we recognize that there is more work to be done, and with that in mind, we offer some concluding reflections on what we will do differently in our own future inquiry in the hopes that it will be useful to other researchers who take up these issues.

Earlier, we mentioned the challenges we faced in ensuring that our data were consistent across and within schools. Because our initial sampling approach was based on student enrollment in particular courses, we had limited control over who qualified for the study. In future endeavors, rather than basing our sample on school-defined factors—which can be unpredictable and largely out of our control—we would employ more "theoretical sampling"—that is, interviewing the most tech-savvy students to find out how their interests and experiences came about. Of course, targeting these students, as we have learned in this study, requires identifying these students and encouraging them to participate in an interview or focus group.

Second, although our data collection timeline in this project was generous, we nevertheless longed for more time with the students. Our one-on-one interviews yielded incredible insights, but we were aware that with more time, we might have learned even more. In future studies we would ensure the time and resources for as much—or perhaps even more—time to investigate the problem. This would allow us not only to gather more observational data but also to build greater trust with individual students and their educators. By the same token, in future research we will likely utilize survey instruments and questionnaires to supplement the qualitative instruments to gather background information from our informants, rather than including it in interview questions as we did in this study. This approach not only saves time but also facilitates consistency in data collection.

We have also resolved that to the extent possible, matching interviewee and interviewer on race and gender (and even relative age) is critical at the high school level, particularly when the conversation is centered on sensitive issues. While our team was diverse, it was not sufficiently diverse to consistently match interviewee and interviewer, as we would have preferred. As we were knee-deep in our data collection, we discussed these challenges with our advisory committee, and from that conversation emerged the idea to conduct focus groups. As one of our advisers pointed out, these are the types of issues that necessitate safe places, with other kids from like backgrounds. Focus groups serve this purpose well because they allow conversations to develop from the group as a whole—rather than from an "outsider"—and as a result, often encourage a greater comfort level among the participants. These discussions actually turned out to be one of our most successful research approaches in terms of being able to talk about race, largely—we believe—because the students felt more at ease in the company of each other and the teachers they trusted. As we continue our investigations into underrepresentation in computer science, we will most certainly include focus group discussions in our methodological approaches.

In terms of our data analysis, we are aware that for every qualitative coding and analysis choice there is a trade-off—gains and costs. The strategy we devised allowed us the greatest degree of confidence in our findings, but it is, we believe, weighted in the institutional direction, sharply illuminating structural issues, and sometimes at the expense of individual life stories. We believe that one reason our data spoke more clearly to broader structural issues is the set of logistic constraints we have already addressed: it is difficult for many people to talk about issues of race, gender, and inequity; high school students of color who are rushed through interviews with unfamiliar (often white) strangers from an outside organization most certainly felt this discomfort (or reluctance) several times over. But more broadly speaking, this focus reflects the powerful life-shaping influence that institutional norms and structures have on the individual trajectories and "decisions" of high school students, especially in low-resourced schools with large numbers of students of color. Future research should seek to strike a balance between the structural and the individual; the size of the sample and the ability to go deeper with individuals.

Finally, we remain curious about best practices, and who is getting it right. One question that we are eager to explore is where, in comparable schools, computer science instruction is going well. What are the ingredients for success? Locating the success stories, and understanding more about their history and what sustains them, has the potential to illuminate so much that we still need to learn.

# Notes

## Introduction

1. The Center for Disease Control's "Water-Related Injuries: Fact Sheet" (<http://www.cdc.gov/ncipc/factsheets/drown.htm> [accessed November 8, 2007]) reports that "between 2000 and 2004, the fatal unintentional drowning rate for African Americans overall was 1.3 times that of whites. However, in certain age groups it was even higher. For example, the fatal unintentional drowning rate for 5–14 year old African Americans was 3.2 times higher than that for whites." The fact sheet's discussion on groups at risk states that "factors such as the physical environment (e.g., access to swimming pools) and a combination of social and cultural issues (e.g., valuing swimming skills and choosing water-related activities when making recreational choices) may contribute to the racial differences in drowning rates. If minorities participate less in water-related activities than whites, their drowning rates (per exposure) may be higher than currently reported."

2. In all cases, we use pseudonyms when we quote students in order to protect their identities. We have given most of the teachers we quote pseudonyms as well. In our later discussion of our summer institute, with the participants' permission, we use the teachers' real names.

3. "Out of the Loop; Why Are So Few Underrepresented Minority High School Students Learning Computer Science?" (EIA-0090043) and "Constructing the Computer Science Pipeline: How High School Structures and Norms Narrow Access to Computer Science for Underrepresented Minority Students" (EIA-0213662).

4. According to the Computing Research News, the percentage of incoming undergraduates among all degree-granting institutions who indicated they would major in CS declined by 70 percent between fall 2000 and 2005 (Vegso 2007). This data is based on the CIRP Freshman survey from the Higher Education Research Institute at the University of California at Los Angeles <www.gseis.ucla.edu/heri/freshman.html>. The Computing Research Association's analysis of this downward trend can be found in the "Low Interest in CS and CE Among Incoming Freshmen," a CRA Bulletin posted February 6, 2007 by Jay Vegso (<http://www.cra.org/wp/index.php?p=104>, accessed January 15, 2008). For

statistics on the intentions of first-year college students to major in computer science by race and gender, see <http://nsf.gov.statistics/wmpd/pdf/>. Between 2002 and 2005, high school Advanced Placement computer science test takers nationwide decreased by 19 percent (College Entrance Examination Board 2002 and 2005).

5. A debate between policymakers about the extent of the shortage of computing and engineering expertise in this country is under way. Regardless of the extent of this shortage, the underrepresentation in the field along with the need to improve the quality of mathematics, science, computer science, and engineering education in this country especially in low-income schools with high numbers of students of color is uncontested. For more on the debate, see Monastersky (2007).

6. Robert Moses is the recipient of a MacArthur Foundation Fellowship for his work on mathematics and science literacy.

7. See Apple (1990). Education theorist Michael Apple argues that high-status knowledge in corporate societies is the knowledge necessary to keep these economies operating at a high level. Because the generation of this knowledge largely takes place in the universities, high-status knowledge in secondary schools is largely that which prepares students for and provides access to the universities and eventual high-status jobs.

8. Stanford University Computer Science Education, "Undergraduate User's Guide," available at <http://cse.stanford.edu/resources/users-guide/01.html> (accessed July 9, 2007; link now discontinued).

9. For more discussion on what computer science is and its interdisciplinary connections, see Computer Science Teachers Association (2003, 2005).

10. See Carnegie Mellon School of Computer Science's Center for Computational Thinking, available at <http://www.cs.cmu.edu/computational_thinking.html> (accessed November 8, 2007).

11. For more of Jeannette Wing's thoughts on this issue, see her remarks before the Computer and Information Science and Engineering's Distinguished Education Fellow Award Ceremony, NSF, Arlington, VA, July 13, 2007, available at <http://www.nsf.gov/events/event_summ.jsp?cntn_id=109935&org=CISE> (accessed November 8, 2007).

12. For more information, see, for example, Sargent (2004).

13. An essay by Steven Lohr (2006) cites biology as an example of a discipline that is now able to explore new territory because of computing. The article discusses work by University of California at Berkeley professor Richard Karp, who argues that science is increasingly studying dynamic processes and using algorithms to describe them, as opposed to static phenomena that are more suited to equations and formulas. Since computer science is the systemic study of algorithms, Karp explains how scientists now seek to describe the biological processes, like protein production, as algorithms, and biology is now understood as an information science. "In other words," Karp notes, "nature is computing."

14. We also appreciate Beverly Daniel Tatum's discussion (2007, especially chapter 4) of the implications of technological advances for democracy.

15. The demographic breakdown of the Los Angeles Unified School District is the following: Hispanic (73.3 percent), black (11.2 percent), white non-Hispanic (8.9 percent), Asian (3.8 percent), Filipino (2.2 percent), Pacific Islander (0.3 percent), and American Indian (0.3 percent). For LAUSD five-year demographics, see ‹http://lausd.k12.ca.us/lausd/offices/bulletins/5_year_review.html›.

16. For a discussion of our research findings around the important issue of gender and pre-college computing, see Barker et al. (2006); Cohoon and Aspray (2006); and Goode, Estrella, and Margolis (2006). For an in-depth exploration of gender issues in computer science at the postsecondary level, see Margolis and Fisher (2002).

17. These schools tend to be smaller learning communities and/or well resourced. Within the LAUSD, smaller learning communities are currently being established within larger overcrowded schools, and some will be based on a mathematics, science, and technology theme. This could be an opportunity to establish curriculum in a more innovative way.

18. According to the California Department of Education, students from a family of four, with a family income of $37,000 and under, qualify for free and reduced-cost lunch programs.

19. For more information on the *Williams v. State of California* lawsuit, see <http://www.decentschools.org>. For information on graduation rates, see University of California Accord (2006).

20. The Digital High School legislation, enacted in 1997, allocated $1 billion over four years to offer computers and Internet access to California's high schools. The goal of the legislation was to provide "all high school students with basic computer skills," and "improve academic achievement in all subject areas" (Schiff and Solomon 1999).

21. We are deeply grateful to Claude Steele, who was a member of our research advisory committee. It was in conversation with him about segregation in different activities, and how this segregation becomes normalized and naturalized, that our attention to these issues was crystallized. Other works that we have found useful in this are discussed more in chapter 5.

22. Scylla and Charybdis, two sea monsters of Greek mythology, are situated on opposite sides of a narrow channel of water, so close that sailors avoiding Charybdis will pass too close to Scylla and vice versa. The phrase "between Scylla and Charybdis" has come to mean being in a state where one is between two dangers, and moving away from one will cause you to be in danger from the other.

23. In chapter 7, we explain in detail why we focused on AP computer science even though we were critical of the AP system and the narrow framework of AP computer science in particular.

24. See Jesse (2006) for an additional discussion of the shortcomings of the pipeline metaphor.

25. On June 28, 2007, the U.S. Supreme Court settled the two cases: *Parents Involved in Community Schools v. Seattle School District No. 1, et al.,* and *Meredith v. Jefferson County Board of Education, et al.*

## Chapter 1

1. In *Born in Bondage,* historian Marie Jenkins Schwartz (2001) reports that slaveholders did not encourage slaves to swim because swimming could be a possible form of escape, might lead to drowning and thereby a loss of property, and did not increase a slave's economic value. Some other historians report evidence of slaves being excellent swimmers, but that they were forced by their owners to use their swimming and diving abilities to do dangerous as well as unpleasant activities, such as pearl diving and other maritime tasks, to generate more revenue for the owners (Dawson 2006). Kevin Dawson argues that "evidence that slaves were strong swimmers raises issues about present-day American society" (25), since swimming is such a white sport.

2. In *Contested Waters,* Wiltse (2007, 188) reports how seventy of the eighty-four pools in New York City were mini-pools—rectangular and measuring only twenty by forty feet. In Chicago, all but one of the thirty-two opened pools were mini-pools.

3. PDR stands for Philadelphia Department of Recreation. In *Pride,* the letters are said to stand for pride, determination, and resistance.

4. According to Lee Pitts, a nationally and internationally known swim instructor, African Americans ended up swimming in unprotected swimming holes historically, and thus parents, understandably concerned about their children's safety, discouraged swimming.

5. See <http://www.cdc.gov/ncipc/factsheets/drown.htm> (accessed November 8, 2007).

6. The article also discusses the response to these disparities in access to swimming pools from Los Angeles county supervisor Yvonne Burke, who founded the Aquatic Foundation of Metro Los Angeles to help support pools in the inner city, including two that are open year-round.

7. Today, African Americans comprise only 5 percent of the swimmers on the thirty-eight teams in the LAUSD.

8. This is an example of how wealthy parents bolster up their schools' programs in ways that are not possible in low-income struggling communities.

9. We concur that studies based on the faulty assumption that there are distinct racial categories with distinct physical differences cannot override the centrality of historical and economic factors in determining access and social acceptance for people of color in different sporting worlds (P. B. Miller, 1998).

10. See Gilchrist et al. (2000) for a discussion of self-reported swimming ability of U.S. adults. Fear of swimming is also discussed by Dr. Christine Branche,

director of the Unintentional Injury Prevention Division at the Center for Disease Control, in the October 2005 issue of Aquatics International.

11. We are grateful to John Cruzat, the diversity specialist for USA Swimming, for his insights about these issues and providing valuable feedback on a draft of this chapter. In an interview with National Public Radio (June 20, 2006 "Diversity at the Swimming Pool") Cruzat discusses historical roots to the fear of swimming. See <http://www.npr.org/templates/story/story.php?storyId=5497905>.

12. A scholar who has studied the underrepresentation of women in science, Sheila Tobias, explains that the "boy wonder syndrome" is part of the ideology of science and who does science—in other words, the belief that both scientific talent and interest come early in life, and if you don't exhibit these qualities early on, you won't be a good scientist. Because fewer girls than boys display these traits, or are encouraged to display them, the culture is one that discriminates by gender. This is discussed in greater detail in Alper (1993).

13. See, for example, <http://www.makeasplash.org>.

## Chapter 2

1. To maintain the confidentiality of the school, this and other school names used in the text are pseudonyms.

2. See California Basic Educational Data Systems data, 2003–2004, available at <http://www.cde.ca.gov/ds/sd/cb/>.

3. East River had an Academic Performance Index score of 557 from 2003 to 2004, placing it in the second decile. These scores range from 200 to 1,000, and all schools and subgroups with scores lower than 800 must meet annual target scores until they reach 800. The No Child Left Behind legislation identifies all schools that do not make Adequate Yearly Progress for program improvement. For more discussion on school program improvement, see <http://www.cde.ca.gov>. For the Academic Performance Index ranking of individual schools, see <http://www.ed-data.k12.ca.us>.

4. Technology was also not integrated into other areas of the school. As of 2004, there was only one certified faculty member, at 0.2 full-time equivalent, who provided technology curricular support to teachers and students, and there was no classified staff supports for educational technology integration in the school (California Department of Education 2005).

5. A loop is a sequence of statements in computer programming that is specified once, but that may be carried out several times in succession until a condition has been met.

6. For further discussion of all the misconceptions about computer science and how these get translated in the high school classroom, how computer science has traditionally been taught, and suggestions for improvement, see Computer Science Teachers Association (2005).

7. East River was a Concept 6 multitracked school, meaning it was devised to address overcrowding. Three tracks rotate through the school year, with two tracks in session at any time, and a third track on "vacation." During the 2004–5 academic year, 130 Concept 6 schools were operated by the LAUSD. As mentioned earlier, these Concept 6 schools were a special focus of attention in a court case (*Williams v. State of California*) filed in 2000 by a group of students and their parents arguing that the California educational system was not meeting its constitutional obligation to educate all students equally. See <http://www.decentschools.org>.

8. The distinction between computer science and computer literacy was so misunderstood throughout the LAUSD that we needed to define and redefine them, over and over again, to both students and educators in all three schools we studied. The Computer Science Teachers Association (2005)has found this misunderstanding to exist nationwide, and works to reeducate educators about what computer science is and what the curriculum should be for the K–12 level.

9. In 1999, California state law authorized the development of the California High School Exit Examination, an examination that California students have to pass to earn high school diplomas. The class of 2006 was the first one required to pass this exit exam.

10. For more on deficit thinking, see Valencia and Solórzano (1997).

11. A policy brief, "Resources for English Learner Education," by Patricia Gándara and Russell Rumberger (2007), discusses how many teachers do not feel competent to teach English learners, and that within the school system, "there is not deep capacity to help teachers acquire these skills." See also Gándara et al. (2003). And for a discussion of what type of schooling could address the needs of English learners, see Gold (2006).

12. For a discussion of the legacy of vocational education as well as the current reforms that are being considered for integrating academic and vocational educational pathways, see Oakes and Saunders (2007). This article reviews the history of vocational education, and summarizes the arguments in a series of articles that examine the need for educational "multiple pathways" that "offer students and their families choices among a variety of high school programs that provide both the academic and the career foundations students need for advanced learning, training, and responsible public participation" (1).

13. The University of California Accord along with the UCLA Institute for Democracy, Education, and Access publishes an annual California Educational Opportunity Report. These reports bring together data citing the state's progress in providing high-quality learning opportunities for California public school students. See also UCLA Institute for Democracy, Education, and Access (2004).

14. For more discussion on the disparities in the access to AP classes, see Brown (2004). See also Solórzano and Ornelas (2002).

15. See <http:/www.calstate.edu/EAP>.

16. Gándara discusses how all of these students had been good students to begin with, "but, without someone interceding at the right moment, by their own admission, many probably would not have followed the educational paths they did" (115–116). She describes how sometimes it was "luck"—meeting the right teacher or having a good mentorship program in the school. Financial aid availability is also a factor.

17. For a discussion of the important role of "care" in schooling, see, for example, Valenzuela (1999).

18. A set of two longitudinal studies found that certain academic resources have a higher impact on competing in higher education than SES. Among the resources, the rigor and intensity of the high school curriculum is most important, accounting for 42 percent of the resources that students bring with them to higher education. See Adelman (1999, 2006). Also, in a qualitative study at Berkeley High School, California, Gilberto Conchas (2001) found that different programs within one school resulted in varied outcomes for Latino students. The general academic program, with low support and expectations from peers and teachers, resulted in low academic achievement; the supportive, challenging, and cooperative Medical Academy led students to become "active agents in the creation of school success" (501). See also Burris and Welner (2005).

19. The College Opportunity Ratios are described and discussed in the University of California Accord Report (2006).

## Chapter 3

1. There is an aerospace, math, and science magnet program at Westward High. Magnet schools are designed to attract students voluntarily from outside the school's immediate neighborhood to increase the racial diversity within the school.

2. These data are derived from the California Basic Educational Data System, available at <http://www.cde.ca.gov/ds/sd/cb/>. The percentages may not sum to 100 percent due to nonresponses, multiple responses, or responses of "other."

3. These data are derived from the California Basic Educational Data System, available at <http://www.cde.ca.gov/ds/sd/cb/>.

4. We were cautious at first to define Westward in any way by hip-hop and basketball, not wanting to erroneously depict a stereotypical "typically black" school, and yet as we interviewed students and teachers at Westward these were confirmed as activities that do indeed distinguish the school for those who work and learn within it.

5. Westward had an Adequate Yearly Progress score of 608 in 2004. Academic Performance Index scores range from 200 to 1,000, and all schools and subgroups with scores lower than 800 must meet annual target scores until they reach 800. The No Child Left Behind legislation identifies all schools that do not make Adequate Yearly Progress for program improvement. For more discussion on school

program improvement, see <http://www.cde.ca.gov>. For the Academic Performance Index ranking of individual schools, see <http:/www.ed-data.k12.ca.us>.

6. The five students in the class were Russian (two), African American (one), Indian (one), and white (one).

7. For a discussion of how schools are filled with language that "continue[s] to make race and to build racial orders," even when it is "muted" and indirect, see Pollock (2004).

8. Sociocultural scholars Jean Lave and Etienne Wenger have researched the importance of informal learning communities, referred to as "communities of practice" (see, for example, Wenger 1998). This reduction in access reminds us of what Mark Warschauer (forthcoming) found in a study of laptop programs: "Two of the low-SES schools forbade their students from taking computers home, whereas all of the high-SES schools in [the] study allowed students to take laptops home."

9. For more discussion on the ways that the nerd identity is and is not part of the normative gatekeeping for participation in fields such as computer science, see Eglash (2002).

10. The "facilitators" frame is presented in Raymore (2002).

11. These ideas are also explored by John C. Phillips (1976, 49), who argues that "good black athletes are concentrated in those sports in which blacks in general have access (in terms of coaching, facilities, and competition). Good white athletes are dispersed across more sports because they have access to a wider variety of sports." Also, David Ogden (2002) interviewed twenty-seven youth baseball coaches from six states about the underrepresentation of minorities on baseball teams. In addition to the lack of those "facilitator" factors cited for basketball, the most common reasons for the lack of racial diversity in baseball were the paucity of facilities in black neighborhoods, the cost of playing the game, the lack of parents' interest in the sport, and the lack of community support.

12. As Ronald E. Hall (2002, 115; as cited in Ogden and Hilt 2003) contends, "While legitimate science has yet to conclude whether Black athletes possess innate physical qualities, the White basketball player performs in a world that is apparently already convinced of the stereotype." Further, he argues that the over-performance of African Americans and the underperformance of whites in this sport can be attributed to expectations and stereotypes that presume that blacks possess innate qualities that assure their superiority.

13. These findings concur with the studies identifying Asians as being thought of the "model minority" (Lee 1996).

14. For an instructive article about stereotypes and how they get automatically activated, see Blasi (2002), which discusses how many social issues are "race-coded" and trigger associations even when the discourse is "color-blind." For example, welfare is associated with laziness among blacks, crime is associated with blacks and Latinos, and urban signifies minorities in general. See also Krieger (1995).

15. For an important discussion about academic identity and African American students, see Perry, Steele, and Hilliard (2003). In her essay in this volume, "Competing Theories of Group Achievement," Theresa Perry discusses the critical role of schools in continually challenging the widespread societal views that insist on African American intellectual incompetence. To counter these prevalent views, schools must be places of high expectations and rigorous curriculum: "If African American children and youth are to achieve at high levels and be able to see and experience themselves as intellectually competent, they need an intellectually challenging curriculum. To tell students that they are smart and to repeatedly teach content that is not intellectually challenging affirms that in reality the students are not seen as smart or intellectually capable" (Perry 2003, 103).

16. Professor Carol Dweck, in the early 1980s, found that there are two competing views of intelligence: one that it is fixed and innate, and the other that it is malleable and can change with effort. Her research on this subject also showed that students are more motivated to achieve when they believe that intelligence is malleable. See, for example, Dweck (1986). For additional research on this subject, refer to studies done by Carol Dweck, Joshua Aronson, and Catherine Good. See also <http://www.reducingstereotypethreat.org>.

17. Advanced mathematics courses are those beyond algebra, the fourth- or fifth-year high school mathematics including trigonometry/precalculus or AP calculus.

18. These statistics were obtained from the California Department of Education Data Quest, available at <http://dq.cde.ca.gov/Dataquest>.

19. University of California Accord Report (2006).

20. The College Opportunity Ratios are described in the University of California Accord Report (2006).

## Chapter 4

1. These data are derived from the California Basic Educational Data System, available at <http://www.cde.ca.gov/ds/sd/cb/>. The percentages may not sum to 100 percent due to nonresponses, multiple responses, or responses of "other."

2. While Asian males are not underrepresented in college-level computer science or the computer science industry, in this particular school class there were few Asian students. Our discussion therefore focuses on white students as the majority.

3. In a series of articles about the narrowness of the status quo curriculum, computer science educators Judith Gal-Ezer and David Harel (1998, 82) call for high school programming classes to be taught in a broad sense, "covering not only the coding act itself, but also the design of the algorithms underlying the programs and, to some extent, considerations of correctness and efficiency." But this rarely happens.

4. For a comprehensive discussion of these issues, see the Computer Science Teachers Association (2005).

5. We received a separate grant to provide all of the teachers in our study with some financial resources to help them with program implementation. As part of this grant, teachers met with us on a quarterly basis to discuss our findings, and give us deeper insight into their schools and the problem of segregation within them.

6. Only one student in our Canyon study reported not having a home computer. This student had to go to his aunt's house if he wanted to use a computer, one that he had to share with his cousins, who also needed it to complete homework assignments.

7. See Lazarus, Wainer, and Lipper (2005).

8. There were four focus group meetings, two for the AVID class, and two for the MESA class. Both classes had about eighteen to twenty students each.

9. For a comprehensive review of the research on stereotype threat, see Steele (2003).

10. This effect is not just for students of color or females in arenas that are traditionally dominated by white males. It was also witnessed in white males as they compare themselves in math, an arena where Asian males are presumed to excel. See, for example, Aronson et al. (1999).

11. PBS *Frontline* interview with Claude Steele, available at <http://www.pbs .org/wgbh/pages/frontline/shows/sats/interviews/steele/html>.

12. The Posse Foundation is one such organization. This program "identifies, recruits and trains dynamic urban public high school students and sends them to elite colleges and universities in multicultural teams," in order to increase their academic success. The Posse Foundation president and founder, Deborah Bial, was awarded a 2007 MacArthur "Genius" grant for her work. See <http://www .possefoundation.org>. Other programs that also work with cohorts of students are the Meyeroff Scholars Program (<http://www.umbc.edu/meyeroff//>) and the Workshop/Emerging Scholars Program directed by Professor Uri Treisman at the University of Texas at Austin.

# Chapter 5

1. This work never could have occurred without the active involvement and support of several LAUSD divisions. The financial support for substitute teachers, buses, and teacher stipends were all provided by the LAUSD. The LAUSD endorsers were the director of secondary science, the Office of Instructional Technology, the director of mathematics education, the director of the Gifted and Talented Program, and the director of the College Readiness Program. The 2005 and 2006 institutes were part of an official LAUSD memorandum distributed to all principals.

2. The national breakdown of the 2007 AP computer science test takers is as follows: males 83.3 percent, and females 16.7 percent; whites 63.3 percent (males 55.3 percent, and females 8.0 percent); Asians 25.4 percent (males 19.4 percent,

and females 6.0 percent); Latino/as 7.0 percent (males 5.4 percent, and females 1.6 percent); African Americans 3.9 percent (males 2.8 percent, and females 1.1 percent); and American Indians 0.4 percent (males .3 percent, and females 0 percent—only 9) (College Entrance Examination Board 2007).

3. For discussions about the importance of situating teaching instruction within the culture of a community, see Luis C. Moll and colleagues (1992). This work argues that teachers must capitalize on the "funds of knowledge" that students have from their homes and communities to enhance teaching and learning.

4. For a discussion of socially relevant computing, see the work of Michael Buckley at <http://www.cs.buffalo.edu/~mikeb/>. The Computer Science Unplugged curriculum, which began as a way to teach computer science concepts without the benefit of a computer, is also a way to make the teaching of computer science more fun, engaging, and up-to-date, and show that it can always be contextualized for a particular community of learners to make it even more engaging. See <http://csunplugged.com/index.php/activities>.

5. California, like many other states, does not offer a computer science teaching credential. Instead, California places computer science as a topic associated with a business teaching credential. For more discussion on these credentialing issues, see Computer Science Teachers Association (2006).See also Stephenson (2005).

6. Due to a shortage of funding, subsequent summer institutes (after 2005) were of a smaller scale and offered for one week each summer instead of two.

7. This program, which is a partnership between the LAUSD and UCLA's Graduate School of Education and Information Studies, provides enrichment instruction for LAUSD mathematics and science AP students and teachers.

8. Unfortunately, we have not had the funding to conduct any formal interviews with the students who attend the AP Readiness program or to track their progress. This is a loss, for we believe that these students' stories are critical to know as we attempt to find more strategies about what works for broadening the participation in computing. We hope to raise the necessary funds to be able to conduct this research.

9. The AP audit required schools to submit an application that specified that the curricular and resource requirements of the College Board were represented in each AP course offered at the school. AP teachers were required to supply their syllabi outlining the courses' topics and assessments as well as a completed application in order to teach a class approved by the College Board beginning in the 2007–8 school year.

10. Immediately after the institute, teachers voiced their urgent need to secure a curriculum developed specifically for the AP computer science course. Prior to the institute, the teachers had been provided a Java-based curriculum, but the materials did not focus specifically on the AP Java subset, nor was it written for high school students.

11. There are approximately two hundred thousand high school students in LAUSD schools.

12. This teacher is identified with a pseudonym.

13. In fact, we have not been successful in involving East River or Westward in our teacher programs.

14. See Maloney et al. (2008) for a discussion of Computer Clubhouse, innovative programs teaching programming to urban youth.

15. Funding is always an issue in projects such as this, and it is important to note how much our work and others' rely on external grant funding to establish and sustain successful programs. The length of many grants is one to three years, and often more time than that is required to establish programs, gather evidence of effectiveness, and create systemic change.

16. Beginning in 2007–8, our new project, "Into the Loop: A University-K–12 Alliance to Increase and Enhance the Computer Science Learning of African American, Latino/a, and Female Students in the Second-Largest School District in the Country," has been funded by the Broadening the Participation in Computing division of the NSF's Computer and Information Science and Engineering. Our partners are the LAUSD and the UCLA Center for Embedded Network Sensing.

17. As we initiate a local university/K–12 partnership to design an innovative computer science course that will engage students with the foundational principals of computer science, we will partner with local educators and national organizations who have long been addressing this need and who are dedicated to the same goals, including the ACM Education Committee, the Computer Science Teachers Association, Georgia Computes (Yardi and Bruckman, 2007), and Building Bridges Project (Lester 2007), to name a few. See also Roberts 2004.

18. Fullan (1993, 3) describes teachers' inquiry as the continuous and persistent questioning of direction and purpose; it is the kernel of teachers as lifelong learners.

19. For the Computer Science Teachers Association, see <http://www.csta.acm .org>. For the National Center for Women in Technology, see <http://www .ncwit.org>. For the NSF's Broadening Participation in Computing division, see <http://www.nsf.gov>.

20. Industry has sponsored workshops and Web sites for K–12 teachers. One project, CS4HS, with support from Google, has the goal "to reach out to high school (and K–8) teachers to provide resources to help them teach computer science principles to their students in a fun and relevant way." CS4HS has been initiated by the Carnegie Mellon School of Computer Science, and has the goal of being established at many different universities. See <http://www.cs.cmu.edu/ cs4hs/>. Microsoft, Intel, and other companies also have initiated K–12 outreach efforts.

21. See <http://www.cc.gatech.edu/gacomputes>.

22. For an important historical review of school reform, including a discussion of how much of it has been ignorant of the situation of teachers in their distinct locales and the tension inherent in the systemic change that is necessary, see Tyack and Cuban (1997).

## Chapter 6

1. Other studies that have found that technology has not altered the inequalities in the schools and in some ways has benefited the most privileged, see Schofield Davidson (2002); Warschauer (2006b); Warschauer, Knobel, and Stone (2004). For an analysis of how computers are underused in the schools, see Cuban (2001).

2. This archival material is available at <http://www.ed.gov/pubs/NatAtRisk/risk.html>. Not surprisingly, this type of rhetoric based on the U.S. competitive spirit continues to exist in more recent policy initiatives aimed at improving America's global standing, such as the aptly named American Competitiveness Initiative. See <http://www.whitehouse.gov/stateoftheunion/2006/aci/>.

3. Computer science for high school students, in *A Nation at Risk*, is defined as equipping graduates to: understand the computer as an information, computation, and communication device; use the computer in the study of the other basics as well as for personal and work-related purposes; and understand the world of computers, electronics, and related technologies. See <http://www.ed.gov/pubs/NatAtRisk/recomm.html>.

4. California Assembly Bill 64 created the Digital High School Education Technology Grant Act of 1997 to provide all California public high schools with a technology installation grant within four years and to provide ongoing support and staff training grants. By means of a random selection process for schools with grades 9-12, the bill would provide installation grants of up to $300 per-pupil to purchase computer technology and ongoing grants of up to $45 per-pupil for staff development and maintenance. Participating districts would be required to match grant funds with their own resources. Due to the fiscal crisis in California, the Digital High School funds were cut in 2002, and the program is now defunct in 2008.

5. As noted in Light (2001), according to the National Assessment of Educational Progress, it is students of color who use calculators at the highest rates, and yet they continue to have the lowest mathematical performance in the schools and on standardized tests (Loveless 2000).

6. The program is called the Maine Learning Technology Initiative. See <http://www.maine.gov/mlte/>.

7. For a review of these studies to date, see Warschauer (2006a, 2006b, forthcoming).

8. See <http://www.bls.gov/oes/current/oes_nat.htm#b27-0000>.

9. These data also illustrate what social reproduction theorists note about schooling: it is often hoped to be the "great equalizer," yet "schools actually reinforce social inequality while pretending to do the opposite" (McLeod 1987, 11). See also Anyon (1981).

10. For an exception to this, see the National Research Council Committee on Information Technology Literacy (1999, 2–3) report, which addresses the

importance of both learning beyond rudimentary computer literacy skills and learning foundational concepts of computer science—the basic principles that underpin the technology.

11. For a discussion contrasting our current test-prep curriculum this type of curriculum to some of the other higher-achieving countries, such as Japan, China, and Canada, which each manage their assessment system differently, yet "have in common a curriculum focused on critical thinking, and problem solving," see Darling-Hammond 2007b.

12. See <http://www.ed.gov/about/offices/list/os/technology/plan2004/plan>.

13. In April 2004, the LAUSD issued a district memorandum updating the 1999 Board of Education computer literacy requirements (reference guide no. REF- 913). Beginning with the graduating class of 2004, students were supposed to demonstrate computer literacy in grades six through twelve in order to graduate from high school. These standards include basic word processing and Internet searching skills.

14. These directives are often referred to as the "Gathering Storm" reports. They are responding to the worry that "the scientific and technical building blocks of our economic leadership are eroding at a time when other nations are gathering strength," and argue that improving K–12 science and mathematics education is the number one recommendation for increasing the U.S. talent pool. See the National Academies Committee on Science, Engineering, and Public Policy report, "Rising above the Gathering Storm: Energizing and Employing America for a Brighter Economic Future," available at <http://www.nap.edu/catalog.php?record_id=11463#toc>.

15. See <http://www.whitehouse.gov/stateoftheunion/2006/aci/>.

16. The study was of the Jackson and Austin school districts, examining the Mississippi Subject Area Testing Program (SATP) and the Texas Assessment of Knowledge and Skills (TAKS) tests, respectively. The name of the study is "'Its Different Now': How Exit Exams Are Affecting Teaching and Learning in Jackson and Austin."

17. This model of three dimensions of reform presented by Oakes and Rogers (2006) came out of many years of de-tracking studies and has been instrumental in our work.

18. For example, the NSF's Broadening Participation in Computing program seeks to develop innovative approaches—in collaboration with the computing community—to recruiting and retaining traditionally underrepresented students at the undergraduate and graduate levels. This effort is directed at increasing the participation of African American and Latino/a students as well as American Indians, Alaska Natives, Native Hawaiians, and Pacific Islanders. The Computer Science Teachers Association is also taking a lead in these attempts through its work with K–12 educators.

19. The *Daniels v. State of California* case before the State Superior Court was a civil rights class action suit on behalf of California public high school students

over the lack of access to AP classes in their schools as well as the lack of support from the high school to enroll in AP classes and take AP exams. See Oakes, Rogers, and McDonough et al. 2000.

## Conclusion

1. NCWIT is an alliance of academic, industry, K–12, and social science partners who came together in 2003 "to ensure that women's knowledge and skills are fully represented in the creation, development, and consumption of information technology." The outreach of NCWIT concerns all issues that impact this mission, including educational improvement, the image of computer science, and national policy. See <http://www.NCWIT.org>.

2. The official White House summary of the American Competitiveness Initiative states: "By improving the quality of math, science, and technological education in our K–12 schools, thus engaging every child in rigorous courses that teach important analytical, technical, and problem-solving skills, we will prepare our citizens to compete more effectively in the global marketplace." See <http://www .whitehouse.gov/stateoftheunion/2006/aci/#section5>.

3. *Inequality at the Starting Gate: Social Background Differences in Achievement as Children Begin in School* (Lee and Burkam 2002) shows how students from lower socioeconomic backgrounds (largely students of color) are at a disadvantage before even beginning kindergarten, and that this has lasting effects.

4. The Civil Rights Project/Proyecto Derechos Civiles is located at UCLA, and is codirected by Gary Orfield and Patricia Gándara. It is one of the leading research organizations focused on school resegregation. See <http://www.civilrightsproject .ucla.edu>.

5. There is also a lot to learn from the Pulitzer Prize–winning book that popularized the phrase. *The Best and the Brightest* by David Halberstam (1969) was an investigation into the history of the Vietnam War. Halberstam wanted to figure out how it was that some of the nation's best minds could have gotten us into such a tragic mess. One of the answers was that these "whiz kid" decision makers created their own "echo chamber" and did not hear different perspectives. This is certainly useful for thinking about computer science. What happens when only a narrow band of our population is inventing, exploring, and mastering technology?

6. The two swimmers, both African American, who are likely to participate in the 2008 swim trials for the U.S. Olympic team are Cullen Jones and Maritza Correia. In 2004, Correia was the first African American female to make the U.S. Olympic swim team. The first African American male was Anthony Evans, who won a gold medal in 2000.

7. In an NPR interview about his Nike endorsement, Jones discussed his hope that when other black youths see the campaign, they will be inspired to pursue the sport. See *News and Notes*, September 25, 2006, available at <http://www .npr.org/templates/story/story.php?storyId=6138754>.

## Appendix A

1. Grounded theory is a specific research approach. For more information, see Glaser and Strauss (1967).

2. We draw our inspiration for this from *Speed Bumps* (Weis and Fine 2000), a volume written to reveal the behind-the-scenes ethical and political dilemmas that frequently arise in doing research specifically on race, class, and gender.

3. "Out of the Loop: Why Are So Few Underrepresented Minority High School Students Learning Computer Science?" award number 0090043 (CNS); "Constructing the Computer Science Pipeline: How High School Structures and Norms Narrow Access to Computer Science for Underrepresented Minority Students," award number 0213662 (CNS).

4. MESA is a statewide outreach program administered by the University of California, providing academic support services to more than 24,400 students in California. AVID is another student support program that helps students through instruction of study skills and strategies.

5. This dynamic is also discussed in Weis and Fine (2000, 22). For instance, informants' stories are saturated with evidence of race, and yet they often pledge the irrelevance of race/ethnicity and gender, saying, "I don't think about it much."

# References

Adelman, Clifford. 1999. *Answers in the toolbox: Academic intensity, attendance patterns, and bachelor's degree attainment*. Washington, DC: U.S. Department of Education.

Adelman, Clifford. 2006. *The toolbox revisited: Paths to degree completion from high school through college*. Washington, DC: U.S. Department of Education.

Alper, Joe. 1993. The pipeline is leaking women all the way along. *Science* 16 (260): 409–411.

Amsden, Alice, and Jon C. Clark. 1999. Software entrepreneurship among the urban poor: Could Bill Gates have succeeded if he were black? . . . or impoverished? In *High technology and low-income communities: Prospects for the positive use of advanced information technology*, ed. Donald Schön, Bish Sanyal, and William J. Mitchell, 213–234. Cambridge, MA: MIT Press.

Anyon, Jean. 1981. Social class and school knowledge. *Curriculum Inquiry* 11 (1): 3–41.

Appiah, K. Anthony. 2000. Racial identity and racial identification. In *Theories of race and racism*, ed. Les Back and John Solomos, 607–615. London: Routledge.

Apple, Michael W. 1990. *Ideology and curriculum*. 2nd ed. New York: Routledge.

Aquatics International. 2005. In the minority. Available at <http://www.aquatics intl.com/2005/oct/0510_minority.html> (accessed November 11, 2007).

Arenson, Karen. 2004. A school with all the elements, including dissent. *New York Times*, June 30. Available at <http://query.nytimes.com> (accessed January 15, 2008).

Aronson, Joshua, Michael J. Lustina, Catherine Good, Kelli Keough, Claude M. Steele, and Joseph Brown. 1999. When white men can't do math: Necessary and sufficient factors in stereotype threat. *Journal of Experimental Social Psychology* 35:29–46.

Association of Computing Machinery (ACM). 2003. A model curriculum for K–12 computer science. Available at <http://www.csta.acm.org/Curriculum/sub/ACMK12CSModel.html> (accessed January 15, 2008).

Atkinson, D., R. Jennings, and L. Livingston. 1990. Minority students' reasons for not seeking counseling and suggestions for improvement. *Journal of College Student Development* 31:342–350.

Barker, Lecia, et al. 2006. Recruiting middle school girls into IT: Data on girls' perceptions and experiences from a mixed-demographic group. In *Women and Information Technology: Research on Underrepresentation*, ed. J. McGrath Cohoon and William Aspray. Cambridge, MA: MIT Press.

Becker, Henry J. 2000. Who's wired and who's not? *Future of Children* 10 (2): 44–75.

Blasi, Gary. 2002. Advocacy against the stereotype: Lessons from cognitive social psychology. *UCLA Law Review* 49:1241.

Bowen, William G., and Derek Bok. 1998. *The shape of the river*. Princeton, NJ: Princeton University Press.

Brown, Richard. 2004. Changes in Advanced Placement test taking in California high schools, 1998–2003. UC/ACCORD Research Report Series (report no. RR-002-0105). Los Angeles: UC/ACCORD.

Bureau of Labor Statistics, U.S. Department of Labor. 2006. *May 2006 occupational employment and wage estimates*. Available at <http://www.bls.gov/oes/current/oes_nat.htm#b00-0000> (accessed November 10, 2007).

Burris, Carol Corbett, and Kevin G. Welner. 2005. Closing the achievement gap by detracking. *Phi Delta Kappan* 86 (8): 594–598.

California Department of Education. 2004. *California basic educational data system*. Available at <http://www.cde.ca.gov/demographics/files/index.html> (accessed September 2007).

California Department of Education. 2005. School accountability report cards. Available at <http://www.cde.ca.gov/ta/ac/sa/> (accessed September 2005).

Callahan, Rebecca M. 2005. Tracking and high school English learners: Limiting opportunity to learn. *American Educational Research Journal* 42 (2): 305–328.

Callahan, Rebecca, and Patricia Gándara. 2004. Nobody's agenda: English learners and post-secondary education. In *Immigrant and English-language learners: Strategies for success*, ed. Michael Sadowski. Cambridge, MA: Harvard Education Press.

Chadwick, Andrew. 2006. *Internet politics: States, citizens, and new communication technologies*. New York: Oxford University Press.

Cohoon, J. McGrath, and William Aspray, eds. 2006. *Women in information technology: Research on underrepresentation*. Cambridge, MA: MIT Press.

Coleman, James S. 1961. *The adolescent society: The social life of the teenager and its impact on society*. New York: Free Press.

College Entrance Examination Board. Various years. *Advanced placement program national summary report*. New York: The College Board.

Computer Science Teachers Association. 2003. Forward to *A model curriculum for K–12 computer science: A model curriculum for K–12 computer science: Final report of the ACM K–12 task force curriculum committee.* New York: Computer Science Teachers Association.

Computer Science Teachers Association. 2006. *A model curriculum for K–12 computer science: Final report of the ACM K–12 task force curriculum committee.* Available at <http://csta.acm.org/Curriculum/sub/ACMK12CSModel.html> (accessed November 7, 2007).

Computer Science Teachers Association Curriculum Improvement Task Force. 2005. *The new educational imperative: Improving high school computer science.* New York: Association for Computing Machinery. Available at <http://www.csta.acm.org/Publications/White_Paper07_06.pdf>.

Conchas, Gilberto Q. 2001. Structuring failure and success: Understanding the variability in Latino school engagement. *Harvard Educational Review* 71:475–504.

Cuban, Larry. 2001. *Oversold and underused: Computers in the classroom.* Cambridge, MA: Harvard University Press.

Culp, Katie, Margaret Honey, and Ellen Mandinach. 2005. A retrospective on twenty years of educational technology policy. *Educational Computing Research* 32 (3): 279–307.

Darling-Hammond, Linda. 1997. *Doing what matters most: Investing in quality teaching.* Washington, DC: National Commission on Teaching and America's Future.

Darling-Hammond, Linda. 1998. Teachers and teaching: Testing policy hypotheses from a national commission report. *Educational Researcher* 27 (1): 5–15.

Darling-Hammond, Linda. 2007a. Evaluating "no child left behind." *Nation.* Available at <http://www.thenation.com/doc/20070521/darling-hammond> (accessed November 10, 2007).

Darling-Hammond, Linda. 2007b. High quality standards, a curriculum based on critical thinking can enlighten our students. *San Francisco Chronicle*, October 14, E3.

Dawson, Kevin. 2006. Enslaved swimmers and divers in the Atlantic. *Journal of American History* 92 (4): 1327–1355.

DeBell, Matthew, and Chris Chapman. 2006. *Computer and Internet use by students in 2003: Statistical analysis report.* Washington, DC: U.S. Department of Education, Institute of Education Sciences. Available at <http://nces.ed.gov/pubsearch/pubsinfo.asp?pubid=2006065> (accessed November 10, 2007).

DeGregory, Lane. 2001. Swimming for their lives. *St. Petersburg Times*, August 5. Available at <http://www.sptimes.com/News> (accessed January 16, 2008).

Dewey, John. 1916. *Democracy and education: An introduction to the philosophy of education.* New York: Free Press.

Dickard, N., ed. 2003. *The sustainability challenge: Taking ed-tech to the next level.* Washington, DC: The Benton Foundation Communications Policy Program & EDC Center for Children and Technology. Available at <http://www.benton.org/publibrary/sustainability/sus_challenge.html> (accessed February 4, 2008).

DuBois, W. E. B. [1903] 1989. *The souls of black folk*. New York: Penguin Books.

Dweck, Carol. 1986. Motivational processes affecting learning. *American Psychologist* 41 (10): 1040–1048.

Eckert, Penelope. 1989. *Jocks and burnouts: Social categories and identity in the high school*. New York: Teachers College Press.

Eglash, Ron. 2002. Race, sex, and nerds: From black geeks to Asian American hipsters. *Social Text* 20, no. 2 (Summer): 49–64.

Ellison, Ralph. 1980. *The invisible man*. 2nd ed. New York: Vintage Books. (Orig. pub. 1952.)

Entine, Jon. 2000. *Taboo: Why Black Athletes Dominate Sports and Why We're Afraid to Talk about It*. New York: Public Affairs.

Estrella, Rachel. 2000. The arts and technology in education. Paper presented to the Digital Coast Roundtable, Culver City, California.

Ford, Faith. 2006. Sink or swim: Racial disparity in swimming not always black and white. *Panama City News Herald*, July 3. Available at <http://www.panama cityswimteam.com/oldsite/Articles/NH-20060703.html> (accessed January 16, 2008).

Fox, Erin. 2005. Tracking U.S. trends. *Education Week* 24 (35): 40–42.

Friedman, Thomas L. 2005. *The world is flat: A brief history of the twenty-first century*. New York: Farrar, Straus and Giroux.

Fullan, Michael G. 1993. Why teachers must become change agents. *Educational Leadership* 50 (6): 12–17.

Gal-Ezer, Judith, and David Harel. 1998. What (else) should CS educators know? *Communications of the ACM* 41 (9): 77–84.

Gal-Ezer, Judith, and David Harel. 1999. Curriculum and course syllabi for high-school computer science program. *Computer Science Education* 9 (2): 114–147.

Gándara, Patricia. 1995. *Over the ivy walls: The educational mobility of low-income Chicanos*. Albany: State University of New York Press.

Gándara, Patricia, and Russell Rumberger. 2007. Resources for English learner education. Policy brief presented at Getting from Facts to Policy: An Educational Policy Convening, Ed Source, Sacramento, CA, October 19. Available at <http://www.californiaschoolfinance.org/portals/0/PDFs/Policy/GandaraRum berger_brief.pdf> (accessed November 9, 2007).

Gándara, Patricia, Russell Rumberger, Julie Maxwell-Jolie, and Rebecca Callahan. 2003. English learners in California schools: Unequal resources, unequal outcomes. *Education Policy Analysis Archives* 11 (36). Available at <http://epaa .asu.edu/epaa/v11n36> (accessed November 7, 2007).

Gilchrist, J., J. J. Sacks, and C. M. Branche. 2000. Self-reported swimming ability in U.S. adults, 1994. *Public Health Reports* 115, nos. 2–3): 110–111.

Glaser, Barney, and Anselm Strauss. 1967. *The discovery of grounded theory*. Chicago: Aldine.

Glionna, John. 2006. Swimming laps around the stereotypes. *Los Angeles Times*, February 21. Available at <http://www.blackathlete.net/artman/publish/article_01580.shtml> (accessed January 16, 2008).

Gold, Norm. 2006. The high school English learners needs. University of California Linguistic Minority Research Institute. Available at <http://www.lmri.ucsb.edu/policy/index> (accessed November 7, 2007).

Goode, Joanna. 2007. If you build teachers, will students come? The role of teachers in broadening computer science learning opportunities for urban youth. *Journal of Educational Computing Research* 36 (1): 65–88.

Goode, Joanna, Rachel Estrella, and Jane Margolis. 2006. Lost in translation: Gender and high school computer science. In *Women in information technology: Research on underrepresentation*, ed. J. McGrath Cohoon and William Aspray. Cambridge, MA: MIT Press.

Gould, Stephen J. 1996. *The mismeasure of man.* 2nd ed. New York: W. W. Norton and Company. (Orig. pub. 1981.)

Grubb, W. Norton. 2007. Life after high school: Taking the education gospel seriously. *Education Week* 33. Available at <http://www.edweek.org/ew/articles/2007/06/12/40grubb.h26.html> (accessed November 10, 2007).

Gutstein, Eric. 2001. Real-world projects. *Rethinking Schools* 15 (3). Available at <http://www.rethinkingschools.org/archive/15-03> (accessed November 13, 2007).

Gutstein, Eric. 2007. So one question leads to another: Using mathematics to develop a pedagogy of questioning. In *Improving access to mathematics: Diversity and equity in the classroom*, ed. Na'ilah Suad Nasir and Paul Cobb. New York: Teachers College Press.

Halberstam, David. 1969. *The Best and the Brightest*. New York: Random House.

Hall, Ronald E. 2002. The bell curve: Implications for the performance of black/white athletes. *Social Science Journal* 39 (91): 113–118.

Harvard Graduate School of Education. 2002. Building difference, breaking it down: Interview with assistant professor Mica Pollock. July 1. Available at <http://www.gse.harvard.edu/news/features/pollock07012002.html> (accessed November 8, 2007).

Helliker, Kevin. 2007. Minorities and the swimming gap. *Wall Street Journal*, March 20. Available at <http//online.wsj.com/article_email/article_print/SB117436411788842030-ImyQjAxMDE3Nz10MDMyNDA2Wj.html> (accessed July 10. 2007).

Hochschild, Jennifer, and Nathan Scovronick. 2003. *The American dream and the public schools*. Oxford: Oxford University Press.

Hugo, Esther. 2004. Rethinking counseling for college: Perceptions of school and counselors' roles in increasing college enrollment. PhD diss., University of California at Los Angeles Graduate School of Education and Information Studies.

Jesse, Jolene. 2006. The poverty of the pipeline metaphor: The AAAS/CPST study of nontraditional pathways into IT/CS education and the workforce. In *Women in information technology: Research on underrepresentation*, ed. J. McGrath Cohoon and William Aspray. Cambridge, MA: MIT Press.

Johnson, George. 2001. All science is computer science. *New York Times*, March 25. Available at <http://www.cs.iastate.edu/all-{\h}science-is-cs.html> (accessed January 16, 2008).

Kao, Grace. 2000. Group images and possible selves among adolescents: Linking stereotypes to expectations by race and ethnicity. *Sociological Forum* 15 (3): 407–430.

Kozol, Jonathan. 1992. *Savage inequalities*. New York: Harper Perennial.

Kozol, Jonathan. 2006. *The shame of the nation: The restoration of apartheid schooling in America*. New York: Three Rivers Press.

Krieger, Linda. 1995. The content of our categories: A cognitive bias approach to discrimination and equal employment opportunity. *Stanford Law Review* 47 (6): 1161–1248.

Lareau, Annette, and Erin M. Horvat. 1999. Moments of social inclusion: Race, class, and cultural capital in family school relationships. *Sociology of Education* 72 (1): 37–53.

Lazarus, Wendy, Andrew Wainer, and Laurie Lipper. 2005. *Measuring digital opportunity for America's children: Where we stand and where we go from here*. Santa Monica, CA: Children's Partnership. Available at <http://www.childrens partnership.org> (accessed January 16, 2008).

Lee, Stacey J. 1996. *Unraveling the "model minority" stereotype: Listening to Asian American youth*. New York: Teachers College Press.

Lee, Valerie E., and David T. Burkam. 2002. *Inequality at the starting gate: Social background differences in achievement as children begin school*. Washington, DC: Economic Policy Institute.

Lee, Valerie E., and Ruth B. Ekstrom. 1987. Student access to guidance counseling in high school. *American Educational Research Journal* 24 (2): 287–310.

Lester, Benjamin. 2007. Robotics' allure: Can it remedy what ails computer science? *Science* 318, no. 5853, 1086–1087.

Levy, Frank, and Richard. J. Murname. 2004. *The new division of labor: How computers are creating the new job market*. Princeton, NJ: Princeton University Press.

Light, Jennifer. 2001. Rethinking the digital divide. *Harvard Educational Review* 71 (4): 710–734.

Lohr, Steven. 2006. Computing, 2016: What won't be possible? *New York Times*, October 31. Available at <http://nytimes.com/2006/10/31/science/31essa.html (accessed January 18, 2008).

Lombana, Judy H. 1985. Guidance accountability: A new look at an old problem. *School Counselor* 32:340–346.

Los Angeles Unified School District. Various years. *Enrollment in APCS courses.*

Loveless, Tom. 2000. *How well are American students learning?* Washington, DC: Brookings Institution.

Luttrell, Wendy. 1997. *School-smart and mother-wise.* New York: Routledge.

MacLeod, Jay. 1987. *Ain't no makin' it: Aspirations and attainment in a low-income neighborhood.* Boulder, CO: Westview Press.

Maloney, John, Kylie Peppler, Yasmin B. kafai, Mitchel Resnick, and Natalie Rusk. 2008. Programming by choice: Urban youth learning programming with Scratch. Paper presented at SIGCSE conference, March 12–15, Portland, Oregon.

Margolis, Jane, and Allan Fisher. 2002. *Unlocking the clubhouse: Women in computing.* Cambridge, MA: MIT Press.

McDonough, Patricia M. 2004. Counseling matters: Knowledge, assistant, and organizational commitment in college preparation. In *Preparing for college: Nine elements of effective outreach*, ed. William G. Tierney, Zoë B. Corwin, and Julia E. Colyar, 69–88. Albany, NY: SUNY Press.

Mehren, Elizabeth. 2002. Derided computer plan clicks with Maine students. *Los Angeles Times*, November 17. Available at <http://maine.gov/mlte/articles/latimes111702.pdf> (accessed January 16, 2008).

Meir, Deborah, and George Wood, eds. 2004. *Many children left behind.* Boston: Beacon Press.

Merriam, Sharan. 1998. Qualitative research and case study applications in education. San Francisco: Jossey-Bass Publishers.

Miller, Patrick B. 1998. Anatomy of scientific racism: Racialist responses to black athletic achievement. *Journal of Sports History* 25 (1): 119–151.

Miller, T. K. 1998. *Secondary school counselor survey: A report on the work environment and characteristics of secondary school counselors.* Alexandria, VA: National Association for College Admission Counseling.

Moll, Luis C., Cathy Amanti, Deborah Neff, and Norma Gonzalez. 1992. Funds of knowledge for teaching: Using a qualitative approach to connect homes and classrooms. *Theory into Practice* 31 (2): 132–141.

Monastersky, Richard. 2007. Researchers dispute notion that America lacks scientists and engineers. *Chronicle of Higher Education* 54, no. 12: A14.

Monson, Robert J., and Duane Brown. 1985. Secondary school counseling: A time for reassessment and revitalization. *NASSP Bulletin* 69 (485): 32–35.

Montoya, Margaret E. 2001. A brief history of Chicana/o school segregation: One rationale for affirmative action. *La Raza Law Journal* 12 (2): 159–172.

Moses, Robert P., and Charles E. Cobb Jr. 2002. *Radical equations: Civil rights from Mississippi to the Algebra Project.* Boston: Beacon Press.

Mossberger, Karen, Caroline Tolbert, and Mary Stansbury. 2003. *Virtual inequality: Beyond the digital divide.* Washington, DC: Georgetown University Press.

Nao, Kim. Forthcoming. Becoming AP: The socialization of students of color to AP English. PhD diss., UCLA Graduate School of Education and Information Studies.

National Center for Education Statistics. 2004. Common core data. Washinton, DC: NCES. Available at <http://necs.ed.gov> (accessed November 10, 2007).

National Commission on Excellence in Education. 1983. *A nation at risk.* Washington, DC: U.S. Department of Education.

National Research Council Committee on Information Technology Literacy. 1999. *Being fluent with information technology.* Washington, DC: National Academies Press.

New Commission on the Skills for the American Workforce. 2006. *Tough choices or tough times.* Washington, DC: National Center on Education and the Economy.

Noguera, Pedro. 2003. *City schools and the American dream.* New York: Teachers College Press.

Nossiter, Adam. 2006. Unearthing a town pool, and not for whites only. *New York Times,* September 18. Available at <http://www.nytimes.com/2006/09/18/US/18pool.html> (accessed January 16, 2008).

Oakes, Jeannie. 1989. Tracking in mathematics and science education: A structural contribution to unequal schooling. In *Class, race, and gender in American education,* ed. Lois Weis, 106–125. Albany: State University of New York Press.

Oakes, Jeannie, and Gretchen Guiton. 1995. Matchmaking: The dynamics of high school tracking decisions. *American Educational Research Journal* 32 (1): 3–33.

Oakes, Jeannie, and Martin Lipton. 2007. *Teaching to change the world.* New York: McGraw-Hill Humanities/Social Sciences/Languages.

Oakes, Jeannie, and John Rogers. 2006. *Learning power: Organizing for education and justice.* New York: Teachers College Press.

Oakes, Jeannie, John Rogers, Patricia McDonough, Daniel Solórzano, Hugo Mehan, and Pedro Noguera. 2000. *Remedying unequal opportunities for successful participation in Advanced Placement courses in California high schools.* An expert report submitted on behalf of the Defendants and the American Civil Liberties Union in the case of *Daniel v. the State of California.* Unpub. report.

Oakes, Jeannie, John Rogers, David Silver, Siomara Valladares, Veronica Terriquez, Patricia McDonough, Michelle Renée, and Martin Lipton. 2006. *Removing the roadblocks: Fair college opportunities for all California students.* Los Angeles: UC/ACCORD and UCLA/IDEA. Available at <htpp://www.ucla-idea.org> (accessed November 10, 2007).

Oakes, Jeannie, and Marisa Saunders. 2007. Multiple pathways: High school reform that promises to prepare all students for college, career, and civic responsibility. University of California at Los Angeles, Institute for Democracy, Education, and Access, Multiple Perspectives on Multiple Pathways Series, paper mp-rr002-0207.

Available at <http://repositories.cdlib.org/idea/mp/mp-rr002-0207> (accessed November 9, 2007).

Oakes, Jeannie, and Amy Stuart Wells. 1997. *Beyond the technicalities of school reform: Policy lessons from detracking schools.* Los Angeles: University of California at Los Angeles Graduate School of Education and Information Studies.

Oakes, Jeannie, Amy Stuart Wells, Amanda Datnow, and Makeba Jones. 1997. Detracking: The social construction of ability, cultural politics, and resistance to reform. *Teachers College Record* 98 (3): 482–511.

Ogden, David C. 2002. Youth select baseball in the Midwest. In *The Cooperstown symposium on baseball and American culture,* ed. William M. Simons and Alvin L. Hall, 322–335. Jefferson, NC: McFarland and Company.

Ogden, David C., and Michael Hilt. 2003. The collective identity and basketball: An explanation of the decreasing number of African Americans on America's baseball diamonds. *Journal of Leisure Research* 35: 213–228.

Oppenheimer, Todd. 2004. The flickering mind: Saving education from the false promise of technology. New York: Random House.

Orfield, Gary, and Chungmei Lee. 2005. *Why segregation matters: Poverty and educational inequality.* Cambridge, MA: Harvard Education Publishing Group.

Pascoe, Sue. 2007. New aquatic center at PaliHi seeks funds. *Palisadian Post,* April 12, 3.

Perez, Leonor X. 2000. The interface of individual, structural, and cultural constructs in Latino parents' effort to support their children in planning for college. PhD diss., University of California at Los Angeles Graduate School of Education and Information Studies.

Perry, Theresa. 2003. Competing theories of group achievement. In *Young, gifted, and black: Promoting high achievement among African American students,* ed Theresa Perry, Claude Steele, and Asa Hilliard III, 52–86. Boston: Beacon Press.

Perry, Theresa. 2007. Afterword to *Can we talk about race?* by Beverly Daniel Tatum. Boston: Beacon Press.

Perry, Theresa, Claude Steele, and Asa Hilliard III. 2003. *Young, gifted, and black: Promoting high achievement among African-American students.* Boston: Beacon Press.

Phillips, John C. 1976. Toward an explanation of racial variations in top-level sports participation. *International Review of Sport Sociology* 11 (3): 39–55.

Pierce, Chester M. 1974. Psychiatric problems of the black minority. In *American handbook of psychiatry,* ed. Silvano Arieti, 512–523. New York: Basic Books.

Pitts, Lee. 2007. Black splash: The history of African-American swimmers. Fort Lauderdale, FL: International Swimming Hall of Fame. Available at <http://www.ishof.org/pdf/black_splash.pdf> (accessed November 10, 2007).

Plank, Stephen B., and Will Jordan. 2001. Effects of information, guidance, and actions in postsecondary destinations: A study of talent loss. *American Educational Research Journal* 38 (4): 947–979.

Pollock, Mica. 2004. *Colormute: Race talk dilemmas in an American school.* Princeton, NJ: Princeton University Press.

Rampersad, Arnold. 1998. *Jackie Robinson: A biography.* New York: Ballantine Books.

Raymore, Leslie A. 2002. Facilitators to leisure. *Journal of Leisure Research* 34:37–51.

Roberts, Eric. 2004. The dream of a common language: The search for simplicity and stability in computer science education. Paper presented at SIGCSE Technical Symposium on Computer Science Education, Norfolk, VA, March 3–7.

Rose, Mike. 2005. *The mind at work.* New York: Viking Penguin.

Sargent, John. 2004. The adequacy of the U.S. S&E workforce: A quantitative perspective. Remarks to the Computing Research Association, February 23. Available at <http://www.cra.org/govaffairs/content.php?cid=22> (accessed November 10, 2007).

Schiff, Tamara, and Lewis Solomon. 1999. California Digital High School: Process evaluation, year one report. Prepared for the Milken Family Foundation for the California Department of Education. Available at <http://www.ctap3.org/grants/research.html> (accessed January 18, 2008).

Schoch, Deborah. 2007. A deep tide of good will at Bruce's Beach. *Los Angeles Times*, March 31. Available at <http://www.calcoast.org/news/localgovernment0000004.html> (accessed January 18, 2008).

Schofield, Janet, and Ann Davidson. 2002. *Bringing the Internet to school: Lessons from an urban district.* New York: Jossey-Bass Publishers.

Schwartz, Jenkins Marie. 2001. Born in bondage: Growing up enslaved in the antebellum south. Cambridge, MA: Harvard University Press.

Seymour, Elaine, and Nancy Hewitt. 1997. *Talking about leaving: Why undergraduates leave the sciences.* Boulder, CO: Westview Press.

Shelburne, Ramona. 2007. Swimming pools offer strokes against stereotype. *LA Daily News*, March 23. Available at <http://www.dailynews.com/portlet/article/html/fragments/print_article.jsp?articleId=5498094&siteId=200> (accessed July 10, 2007).

Slear, Tom. 2002. Combine swimming and diversity and two simple truths emerge: The sport isn't diverse, and there are no quick fixes. *Water colors*—A special *Splash* magazine look at diversity in USA swimming. Available at <http://www.usaswimming.org/USASWeb/ViewMiscArticle.aspx?TabId=515&Alias=Rainbow&Lang=en&mid=850&ItemId=928> (accessed January 17, 2008).

Solórzano, Daniel, Miguel Ceja, and Tara Yosso. 2000. Critical race theory, racial microaggressions, and campus racial climate: The experiences of African American college students. *Journal of Negro Education* 69 (1–2): 60–73.

Solórzano, Daniel, and Armida Ornelas. 2002. A critical race analysis of advanced placement classes: A case of educational inequity. *Journal of Latinos and Education* 1 (4): 215–229.

Solórzano, Daniel, and Tara Yosso. 2000. Toward a critical race theory of Chicana and Chicano education. In *Demarcating the border of Chicana(o)/Latina(o) education*, ed. Carlos Tejeda, Corinne Martinez, and Zeus Leonardo, 35–65. Cresskill, NJ: Hampton Press.

Stanton-Salazar, Ricardo D. 1997. A social capital framework for understanding the socialization of racial minority children and youths. *Harvard Educational Review* 67 (1): 1–40.

Steele, Claude. 1992. Race and the schooling of black Americans. *Atlantic Monthly* 269:68–78.

Steele, Claude. 1997. A threat in the air: How stereotypes shape intellectual identity and performance. *American Psychologist* 52:613–629.

Steele, Claude. 2003. Stereotype threat and African-American student achievement. In *Young, gifted, and black: Promoting high achievement among African-American students*, ed. Theresa Perry, Claude Steele, and Asa Hilliard III, 109–130. Boston: Beacon Press.

Stephenson, Chris. 2005. Entering the forbidden forest of teacher certification. *Computer Science Teachers Association Advocate*. Available at <http://blog.acm.org/archives/csta/2005/07/entering_the_fo.html> (accessed November 10, 2007).

Tatum, Beverly Daniel. 2007. *Can we talk about race?* Boston: Beacon Press.

Taub, Eric. 2003. The "matrix" invented: A world of special effects. *New York Times*, June 3, B1.

Terman, Lewis. 1923. *Intelligence tests and school reorganization*. New York: World Book Company. (Cited in Oakes and Saunders 2007).

Trotter, Andrew. 2007. Getting up to speed. *Education Week* 26 (30): 10–17.

Tucker, Allen, Fadi Deek, Jill Jones, Dennis McCowan, Chris Stephenson, and Anita Verno. 2004. *A model curriculum for K–12 computer science*. New York: Computer Science Teachers Association.

Tyack, David, and Larry Cuban. 1997. *Tinkering toward utopia: A century of public school reform*. Cambridge, MA: Harvard University Press.

Tyre, Peg. 2007. A deep wedge between the races. *Newsweek* (September 20). Available at <http://www.newsweek.com/id/41212> (accessed November 10, 2007).

UCLA Institute for Democracy, Education, and Access. 2004. Separate and unequal 50 years after Brown: California's racial opportunity gap. Available at <http://www.idea.gseis.ucla.edu> (accessed November 10, 2007).

University of California Accord. 2006. *California educational opportunity report: Roadblocks to college*. Available at <http://www.edopp.org> (accessed November 9, 2007).

Valencia, Richard, and Daniel Solórzano. 1997. Contemporary deficit thinking. In *The evolution of deficit thinking: Educational thought and practice*, ed. Richard Valencia, 160–210. Washington, DC: Falmer Press.

Valenzuela, Angela. 1999. *Subtractive schooling: U.S.-Mexican youth and the politics of caring*. New York: State University of New York Press.

Vegso, Jay. 2007. Continued drop in CS bachelor's degree production and enrollments as the number of new majors stabilizes. *Computing Research News* 19, no. 2. Available at <http://www.cra.org/CRN/aricles/march07/vegso.html> (accessed January 15, 2008).

Warschauer, Mark. 2000. Technology and school reform: A view from both sides of the track. *Educational Policy Analysis Archives* 8 (4).

Warschauer, Mark. 2004. *Technology and social inclusion: Rethinking the digital divide*. Cambridge, MA: MIT Press.

Warschauer, Mark. 2006a. Laptops and literacy. Paper presented at the annual meeting of the American Educational Research Association, San Francisco, April.

Warschauer, Mark. 2006b. *Laptops and literacy: Learning in the wireless classroom*. New York: Teachers College Press.

Warschauer, Mark. Forthcoming. Laptops and literacy: A multi-site case study. *Pedagogies*.

Warschauer, Mark, Michele Knobel, and LeeAnn Stone. 2004. Technology and equity in schooling: Deconstructing the digital divide. *Educational Policy* 18 (4): 562–588.

Weis, Lois, and Michelle Fine. 2000. *Speed bumps: A student-friendly guide to qualitative research*. New York: Teachers College Press.

Wells, A. S., J. J. Holme, A. T. Revilla, and A. K. Atanda. In press. *Both sides now: The story of school desegregation's graduates*. Berkeley: University of California Press.

Wenger, Etienne. 1998. *Communities of practice: Learning, meaning, and identity*. Cambridge: Cambridge University Press.

Wilhelm, Maria. 1987. Controversy: In America's pastime, says Frank Robinson, white is the color of the game off the field. *People*, April 27, 46.

Wiltse, Jeff. 2007. *Contested waters: A social history of swimming pools in America*. Chapel Hill: University of North Carolina Press.

Wing, Jeannette. 2006. Computational thinking. *Communications of the ACM* 49 (3): 33–35. Available at <http://www.cs.cmu.edu/~wing/publications/Wing06.pdf> (accessed January 18, 2008).

Yardi, Sarita, and Amy Bruckman. 2007. What is computing? Bridging the gap between teenagers' perceptions and graduate students' experiences. In *ICER'07: Proceedings of the 3rd International Workshop on Computing Education Research*. Atlanta, September 13-15. New York: ACM.

Yonezawa, Susan, Amy Stuart Wells, and Irene Serna. 2002. Choosing tracks: "Freedom of choice" in detracking schools. *American Educational Research Journal* 39 (1): 37–67.

Yoo, Paula. 2005. *Sixteen years in sixteen seconds: The Sammy Lee story.* New York: Lee and Low Books.

Zabala, Dalia, and Angela Minnici. 2007. *"It's different now": How exit exams are affecting teaching and learning in Jackson and Austin.* Washington, DC: Center on Education Policy.

Zarate, Maria Estela, and Harry P. Pachon. 2006. *Gaining or losing ground? Equity in offering Advanced Placment courses in California high schools, 1997–2003.* Los Angeles: Tomás Rivera Policy Institute.

Zinser, Lynn. 2006. Everyone into the water. *New York Times,* June 19, E1, E6.

Zweben, Stuart. 2006. 2004–2005 Taulbee survey. *Computing Research News,* May 2006, 7–17. Available at <http://www.cra.org/statistics/survey/05/05.pdf> (accessed November 10, 2007).

# About the Authors

While we came to this issue with different perspectives and backgrounds, and all possess different appetites for technology, all of our work unites around issues of equality and schooling.

**Jane Margolis** is a qualitative researcher in education whose work for the last fourteen years has focused on the social inequities in computer science education. It was personal experience that really made her committed to these issues. Having worked as one of the first female telephone installers in the 1970s, she experienced how learning opportunities allow interests, previously unknown, to emerge. She became driven to understand more about the entangled web of opportunity, interest, ability, race, gender, and class, and became intellectually as well as personally dedicated to creating equal opportunities for all. Margolis is the coauthor of the award-winning book *Unlocking the Clubhouse: Women in Computing* (MIT Press, 2002).

**Rachel Estrella** received her doctorate from the University California at Los Angeles (UCLA) Graduate School of Education and Information Studies. Her work focus, and passion, is the use of the arts as a tool for social and political empowerment for marginalized communities. She is the author of *The Arts and Technology in Education* (2000), a summary report about the state of new media academies in the LAUSD.

**Joanna Goode** began her career as an AP computer science teacher in an urban high school in Southern California. She then received her doctorate from UCLA, researching the technology knowledge gap of college students and its impact. Goode is now an assistant professor of teaching at the University of Oregon College of Education. Her field of expertise is professional development for teachers, and specifically developing alternative curricula and pedagogy in computer science to engage traditionally underrepresented students. Goode is on the board of the Computer Science Teachers Association and is a member of the Association of Computing Machinery's policy committee.

**Jennifer Jellison Holme** is an assistant professor at the University of Texas at Austin. Her work focuses on the high school final exit exams and the consequences for students of color. She is coauthor of *Both Sides Now* (University of California

Press), a forthcoming book about the long-term impact of school desegregation on graduates of racially mixed high schools.

**Kimberly Nao** received her doctorate from the urban schools division of the Graduate School of Education and Information Studies at UCLA. Her dissertation, "Becoming AP: The Socialization of Students of Color to AP English," examines the experiences of students of color in predominantly white AP classrooms as they relate to culture, socialization, and tracking. She has also been a high school English teacher and continues to work with youths who struggle to negotiate alienating institutions such as schools.

It was this mixture of backgrounds and experiences that went into crafting this book. While we were inspired and helped along the way by so many colleagues and friends, including teachers and administrators in the LAUSD, we take sole responsibility for our ideas, as mentioned in the acknowledgments.

# Index